THE COMING ECLIPSE

Or

The Triumph of Climate Mitigation Over Solar Revolution

Graeme Donald Snooks

I G D S

Institute of Global Dynamic Systems Books
Canberra

First published 2010
by **IGDS Books**
Canberra

© Graeme Donald Snooks, 2010

Printed in the United States of America by CreateSpace

National Library of Australia cataloguing-in-publication data
Snooks, G.D. (Graeme Donald)
    The Coming Eclipse

    Bibliography.

    1. Climate mitigation
    2. Economic revolution
    3. General dynamic theory

    ISBN: 978-0-9808394-0-1

In memory of Daphne May Graham (nee Forman)

1918–2008

Contents

List of Figures

List of Tables

Preface

The Coming Eclipse is a futuristic work, yet a critical one. It is concerned to investigate the ultimate implications of any determined global effort to implement the climate-mitigation policies of the Intergovernmental Panel on Climate Change (IPCC). As is well known, this is the influential international body of scientists who are convinced that climate change is real, that it is largely the outcome of human actions, and that it can and must be reversed through the determined application of economy-changing climate-mitigation policies.

The Coming Eclipse is based on two propositions. The first is that the IPCC could well be correct about the fact and cause of climate change. I have certain reservations, as will be briefly discussed in Chapter 2, but these have not influenced the analysis in this book. For the purposes of this exercise, I accept the science of climate change. The second proposition, however, is that the IPCC is completely wrong about the impact of their climate-mitigation policies on the global economy and on human society. The critical problem is that orthodox economics, which underpins mitigation policy, comprises a body of static, marginal (small-issue-based) theory that is unable to handle the huge dynamic processes involved in the way both climate change and climate mitigation impact on the global economy. In other words, the "science" of climate mitigation is fundamentally flawed. What is required to reliably analyze the future impact of climate mitigation on our world is a general dynamic theory of human society. The employment of such a theory is the core contribution of this book. As we shall see, the cost of the mitigation policies being urged upon the governments of the world, instead of being moderate, is outrageously high – almost 100 times greater by 2100 than that advocated by the militant mitigationists.

This book began life as an essay in October 2008. In February 2009 it was circulated electronically as a working paper by the Global Dynamic Systems Centre – the forerunner of the Institute of Global Dynamic Systems (IGDS), Canberra – attached to the Economics Department, Research School of Social Sciences, Australian National University. In publishing this work with IGDS Books, I have decided not to make any changes in the light of publications that have appeared since it was first written, because none of this work affects my core analysis. The book's purpose is not only to reveal the true costs of climate mitigation – to show that economic and technological eclipse is a real possibility – but also to provide a realistic vision of an alternative future for humanity. But it is a future that will only unfold if we understand the underlying historical processes and have the courage to creatively exploit them.

Even short books incur considerable debts. Accordingly, I wish to thank Huw McKay, Andrew Schuller, and Adrian Snooks for their perceptive comments on an earlier draft, thereby saving me from a number of errors and improving the book's presentation. Also I am grateful to Anton Roux for the enthusiastic support he has given this project, which has resulted in a wider distribution of the initial working paper than would have been otherwise possible. And finally I wish to thank Julie Hamilton for her excellent work in formatting this book and designing the cover. This book is dedicated to the memory of Daphne Graham, my ever-supportive mother-in-law.

GDS of Sevenoaks

Chapter 1
A New Technological Revolution

Mankind currently is not only facing a major environmental challenge, it is embarking on a hugely risky enterprise – that of climate mitigation. This unprecedented global adventure is an attempt to change the nature and shape of human society on the grounds that our traditional market system has failed us. The current enterprise is hugely risky because it is based not on what has happened but on what we are told by "climate-mitigation engineers" might happen. The risk is that a relentlessly determined climate-mitigation program at the global level will lead to the eclipse of the coming Solar Revolution.

THE ESSAY'S ARGUMENT

The essay's argument is simple but powerful, and can be outlined in the following five propositions:

- The science of climate *change* is challenging but compelling, based as it is on an impressive and growing body of expert empirical research. What it shows is that recent climate change is human induced. Hence, further climate change and its mitigation are problems primarily for the social not natural sciences.

- The "science" of climate *mitigation* is nonexistent, because orthodox social science has failed to model the dynamics of human society. And it is the dynamics of human society that will largely determine future climate change.

- Orthodox economics, which has attempted to fill the void, has failed completely. Economic theory is suitable only for the analysis of small, short-run issues that can be accommodated within a static framework – such as the price of a cup of tea – whereas the issue of climate mitigation is one of the biggest and most important issues humanity will ever face, it is long-run in nature, and it can only be adequately handled within a dynamic framework. As orthodox economics has been unable to develop a realist general dynamic theory, its practitioners have been forced to employ simplistic historicist models when analyzing future climate change.

- What we need is a new science of human dynamics. The basis for this new science is provided by the author's dynamic-strategy theory. It is a realist theory in the sense that it has been derived from a long-term, systematic observation of the fluctuating fortunes of both human society over the past 2 million years (myrs) and life over the past 4,000 myrs.

- Economists have massively underestimated the costs of their proposed climate mitigation program aimed at stabilizing greenhouse-gas concentrations, because they have employed the inadequate *static* cost–benefit methodology. This essay takes a very different approach. By estimating the *dynamic* costs – essentially the costs of suppressing the imminent technological revolution that can only be identified in a realist dynamic framework – I have found that total costs will be almost 100 times greater than current estimates by the year 2100. This puts a comprehensive mitigation program totally out of the question. What, then, is to be done? This essay provides the answer.

Even if we accept the climate-change science about the recent relationship between human economic activities and climate change – which I do in this essay – we have no *direct* evidence that this relationship will continue to hold during the remainder of the twenty-first century and beyond. We can only "know" the future *indirectly* through the construction of theoretical models that make persuasive predictions about the behavior of humanity and the outcomes of our activity throughout the course of this century. Our "knowledge" of the future, therefore, is only as good as the ability of our models to anticipate the dynamics of human society over the next three or four generations. Greenhouse-gas concentration calculations cannot be correct if the model of human dynamics is either nonexistent or wrong.

In this essay I argue that the theoretical models, both climatic and economic, that the experts have so far employed to estimate the range of possible future greenhouse-gas concentrations, resulting temperature increases, and costs of both "business as usual" and mitigation/adaptation policies, are totally inappropriate. Indeed, these conventional models have generated future projections that are hopelessly and dangerously wrong. We are told, for example, that the costs of mitigation will amount to "only" about 1 percent of world GDP each and every year (currently around $656.1 billion – only slightly less than the size of Australia's GDP, of $773 billion, for a year), whereas a realist dynamic analysis shows that these costs will amount to 12 percent of world GDP by 2050 and 90 percent by 2100.

If this is so, how could the conventional economic models be so wrong? The answer is that despite their rapidly growing *technical* sophistication, these models are, at their core, exercises in naive historicism and, hence, are examples of what Karl Popper (1957) rightly called "the poverty of historicism" – of assuming that the future, even the distant future, will amount to little more than a repetition of the recent past. Basically these climate-mitigation models extrapolate recent trends in the key climatic and economic variables into the distant future. What's wrong with this? Well, while these models make a variety of assumptions about the ways in which key economic variables – population, living standards, energy use per unit of GDP, and carbon dioxide emissions per unit of energy use – might change over time, they are unable to anticipate any major structural changes — on the relative scale of the Industrial Revolution — that might take place in human society.

Why then are possible future revolutionary changes ignored? Because orthodox economic model-builders have failed to employ a realist general dynamic theory to predict where human society might go in the future and how it might get there. A century is a very long time over which to make projections using simplistic historicist models. Compound interest soon makes nonsense of estimates based on faulty premises. Only with the construction and use of a realist general dynamic theory is it possible to predict and explain probably revolutionary structural change during the course of the twenty-first century, and beyond. The contribution this essay makes to the climate-change debate is the use of such a realist theory to show there is a very high probability that a major technological revolution – which, since the early 1990s I have called the Solar Revolution (Snooks 1996) – will be well underway by the middle decades of the twenty-first century.

The Solar Revolution will have a similar impact on human society in the twenty-first century to that of the Industrial Revolution in the nineteenth century or, indeed, to that of the Neolithic Revolution some 10,000 years ago. The unforeseen but impending Solar Revolution – not to be confused with the planned transition to a "low-carbon" economy proposed by the mitigation engineers who have mistakenly appropriated this term – renders all existing projections concerning future greenhouse-gas emissions and concentrations, climate changes, and costs of both "business as usual" and mitigation, completely redundant. It also exposes the current climate-mitigation program as being not only unnecessary but also highly dangerous, because it will delay, even derail, the emergence of the real Solar Revolution.

It is worth repeating that this essay largely accepts the climate-change (as opposed to the climate-mitigation) science, which has developed rapidly over the past two decades. While there are uncertainties arising from the data and models employed, the fundamental proposition – that human society has played a major role in the climate change experienced since the late 1970s – seems to be well established. While this proposition is qualified in Chapter 2, by placing it within a wider historical perspective, it is largely accepted. What cannot be accepted, however, are the unrealistic historicist models employed by economists to calculate the costs of mitigation and as a basis for framing what will be a disastrous mitigation program. While the science of climate change is well established, there is no reputable science of climate mitigation.

THE UNFORESEEN BUT IMPENDING ECONOMIC REVOLUTION

The general dynamic theory employed in this essay is the "dynamic-strategy" theory that I've been developing in a large number of books and articles over the past couple of decades. It is a transdisciplinary theory that has proven its worth in analyzing the big issues of human society in the social, behavioral, biological and cognitive sciences. This theory – which has been published in scientific journals such as *Complexity* (journal of the Santa Fe Institute) – shows how the human pursuit of survival and prosperity has led not only to the rise and fall of civilizations but also to an exponential technological development path generated by a number of economic revolutions or, what I call, technological paradigm shifts. These include the Paleolithic (hunting) Revolution about 1.6 million years (myrs) ago, the Neolithic (or agricultural) Revolution about 10,600 years ago, and the Modern (or industrial) Revolution about 200 years ago. The interesting feature about this technological development path (and the preceding biological one) is that it is exponential in nature, both in terms of the process of succession and the rate at which it proceeds. The dynamic-strategy theory encompasses these technological paradigm shifts as well as the fluctuating fortunes of the civilizations exploiting them. This theory is also used for predicting the development of the global technological path in the future.

The dynamic-strategy theory, as well as real-world evidence concerning the current exhaustion of the existing industrial technological paradigm, suggest with a high degree of confidence that the new economic revolution – the fourth in the history of humanity – will be well underway by the middle decades of the twenty-first century. As discussed in Chapter 5, the real Solar Revolution will totally transform the sources of, and the ways in which we employ, energy. It will involve a shift from all existing energy technologies spawned by the current industrial technological paradigm – both the dominant fossil-burning technologies and the "low-carbon" alternatives – to technologies directly exploiting the energy of the sun.

The real Solar Revolution will have an unpredictable transforming impact on human society, just as did the three earlier economic revolutions, taking us to even higher technological levels. Because of this, the current pressure exerted by an exhausting technological paradigm on the environment and global climate will be dramatically released. In this event, greenhouse-gas emissions will be equally dramatically reduced, global temperatures will cease to rise and will eventually decline to more "normal" levels, and the perceived need for climate mitigation will evaporate completely. The real Solar Revolution – the predictable outcome of the actual dynamic mechanism underlying human society — will completely resolve the climate-change crisis currently generating so much concern. The only climate-change action we will need to take is remedial action required to repair damage *already done* to the physical and social environment through climate change *actually experienced* prior to the emergence of the Solar Revolution.

It is important to realize that climate mitigation and technological revolution are totally incompatible. *You can have one or the other, but not both.* A full-on, comprehensive climate-mitigation program will delay, even derail, the Solar Revolution during the twenty-first century. As discussed in Chapter 5, a comprehensive climate-mitigation program can only be introduced if the "mitigation engineers" – the radical climate-change scientists and economists – are able to hijack global society and "manage" consumers and producers alike. This program of control is being proposed by mitigation engineers such as Nicholas Stern and his colleagues in the 2007 *Stern Review*, as well as contributors to the mitigation volumes compiled by the IPCC. Governments are required not only to set mitigation goals and manipulate the price mechanism through the imposition of carbon taxes and trading, but also to employ a range of regulations, direct interventions, and targeted "sticks and carrots" to change consumer demand and to engineer a shift to low-carbon technologies.

These command measures will not only distort the working of global and national dynamic mechanisms, but will lock these societies into the old exhausting industrial technological paradigm. This process of "technological lock-in" will delay the occurrence of the new technological paradigm shift until the mitigation engineers lose their influence over national and global public authorities. But if it is not possible to dislodge the mitigation engineers, the global economy will very likely end up like the USSR under the Bolsheviks, who set Russia off on a metaphysically designed path that led to collapse just three generations after embarking on the communist experiment in market manipulation. In the extreme scenario where the mitigation engineers and their green allies become politically entrenched, forming some sort of global directorate, the real Solar Revolution may even be eclipsed. This extreme scenario could lead to the rise of regional strongmen (as in the dying phases of the Roman empire), who would attempt to remove political regimes dominated by mitigationists through military means. Some may even turn to conquest as the only alternative to the stalled process of technological paradigm change in the eternal strategic pursuit.

Certainly the real Solar Revolution will only proceed once climate mitigation has been abandoned. But even then, the cost of this global experiment in economic and social manipulation and management will be very high. It will, as shown by the calculations in Chapter 5, make a mockery of claims that climate mitigation will cost in the vicinity of only 1 percent of world GDP per annum.

WHAT LIES AHEAD?

In Chapter 2 – "The Challenge of Climate-Change Science" – the science of climate change is briefly reviewed and placed in historical context. Apart from a few qualifications, I accept this impressive body of work concerning the *past* association between human economic activities and climate change. Accordingly, there is no need to discuss the literature in any great detail. The irony of the scientific argument that recent climate change is largely human-induced will be clear. As these scientists believe future climate change will depend upon the reaction of, and developments within, human society, climate-change science has nothing further to contribute to the debate.

The way is now open for social scientists to show how human society will respond to this crisis. Never slow to proclaim their expertise, orthodox economists have rushed to fill the void by applying their microeconomic theory of the firm to these global issues. This is equivalent to using a nutcracker when only a steamhammer will do. In Chapter 3 – "The Limitations of Orthodox Economics" – the self-proclaimed expertise of economists on big issues like climate change and the dynamics of human society is evaluated. It is argued that while orthodox economists do have something useful to say about small issues taking place over short periods of time, and which can be analyzed in a static framework, they are unable to illuminate the big issues – like climate change and the future of humanity – unfolding over long periods of time, which can only be analyzed in a dynamic framework. Indeed, not only do they have little to say about these big issues, what they do have to say is both misleading and highly dangerous. As we shall see, neoclassical economics consistently and wantonly ignores the dynamic benefits of human decision making.

We need, therefore, to adopt an entirely new approach to climate change and the future dynamics of human society. Before it is too late. This new approach is explored in Chapter 4 – "The Science of Human Dynamics" – where the dynamic-strategy theory is briefly outlined in plain English. Essentially the dynamic-strategy theory is concerned with the operation of a self-starting and self-sustaining organic system in a world hostile to life. In order to survive and prosper, individuals cooperate in the pursuit of one of four possible dynamic strategies – family multiplication (procreation *and* migration), conquest, commerce, technological change – so as to generate material prosperity by either accessing outside resources or extracting greater productivity from internal resources. This strategic pursuit causes the dominant dynamic strategy to unfold, which in turn gives rise to a changing strategic (or dynamic) demand for a wide range of inputs of a material, institutional, ideational, and cultural kind. As the dominant dynamic strategy is progressively exploited and exhausted, society traverses a wave-like development path. And, at a deeper and global level, the resulting rise and fall of major societies drives an underlying process of technological paradigm transition, or economic revolution. This theory, therefore, shows how the dynamics of human society is generated and how this has shaped an exponential development path for technological paradigm change. It also shows why this theory, in contrast to orthodox economics, can handle the big and vital issues of climate change and the future of humanity. But most importantly, this theory makes it clear that a new economic revolution is imminent.

In Chapter 5 – "Mitigation or Revolution? The Real Costs and Benefits" – the dynamic-strategy theory is employed to calculate greenhouse-gas concentrations together with the dynamic costs and benefits of both "business as usual" and the proposed climate-mitigation program over the course of the twenty-first century. It is shown that the real costs of climate mitigation grow exponentially during the twenty-first century owing to the impact of this artificial program – this command system – in delaying the occurrence of the real Solar Revolution. Instead of being close to zero, these costs are actually close to 100 percent of world GDP by the year 2100. For the same reasons, greenhouse-gas emissions are shown to decline correspondingly rapidly.

The essay concludes with a realist discussion of climate-change policy in Chapter 6 – "What's to be Done?" – which is expected to lead to increased human prosperity and security, together with an improvement in the world's physical environment and climate. Essentially this essay is optimistic about the future of both human society and the natural environment, provided humanity's usual commonsense prevails over the interventionist inclinations of the mitigation engineers – provided the Solar Revolution is not eclipsed by climate mitigation.

Chapter 2

The Challenge of Climate-Change Science

Climate change is an endemic feature of the Earth's natural history. Over at least the past 2,000 myrs there has emerged a regular pattern of long swings in climate – consisting of glacial periods of roughly 100,000 years, separated by warmer periods of around 10,000 years – caused by variations in both solar output and the Earth's orbit. No one disputes this. What is in dispute is whether the climate change we are currently experiencing is unique – unique in terms of its abruptness, rate of change, and causes.

Over the past couple of decades the scientific community – apart from a handful of diehard dissenters – has come to the conclusion that the rate of climate change is unprecedented, that the outcome will be highly dangerous to life on Earth, and that it has been caused largely by human activities, namely the burning of fossil fuels and large-scale deforestation. And, it is argued, because human agents have caused climate change since the late 1970s, we should be prepared to bear the cost of mitigating this dangerous development in the future. Indeed, unless we do so our planet, they claim, will become considerably less life friendly.

THE CONVENTIONAL WISDOM

There is an unprecedented degree of agreement within the international scientific community on this issue. The chief expressions of this scientific consensus are the regular massive reports commissioned by the Intergovernmental Panel on Climate Change – the IPCC – that have appeared in 1990, 1996, 2001 and 2007. While the data have become more extensive and the models more sophisticated in this series of reports, the IPCC's central conclusions have remained largely unchanged. These central conclusions are:

- since the Industrial Revolution, human activities – including the burning of fossil fuels and deforestation – have been largely responsible for the steadily growing concentration of greenhouse gases (such as carbon dioxide) in the atmosphere;

- this steadily growing concentration of greenhouse gases has accelerated in the past three decades; and

- this build-up of greenhouse gases in the atmosphere has been largely responsible for the increase in global temperatures by $0.56°$ to $0.94°C$ between 1906 and 2005 (see Figure 2.1).

These conclusions are considered to be "virtually certain" and "very likely".

Figure 2.1 **Global temperatures, 1840–2000**

Global Temperature Time Series

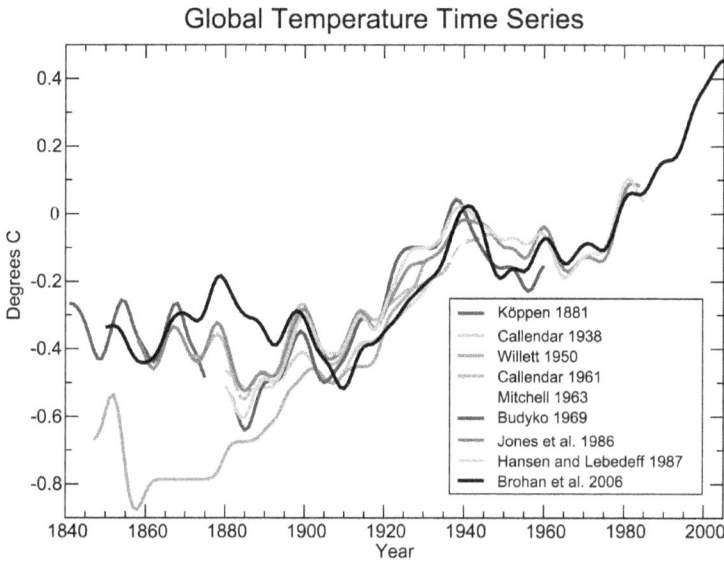

Legend:
— Köppen 1881
    Callendar 1938
    Willett 1950
    Callendar 1961
    Mitchell 1963
— Budyko 1969
— Jones et al. 1986
    Hansen and Lebedeff 1987
— Brohan et al. 2006

Notes: Published records of surface temperature change over large regions. Köppen (1881) tropics and temperature latitudes using land air temperature. Callendar (1938) global using land stations. Willett (1950) global using land stations. Callendar (1961) 60°N to 60°S using land stations. Mitchell (1963) global using land stations. Budyko (1969) Northern Hemisphere using land stations and ship reports. Jones et al. (1986a,b) global using land stations. Hansen and Lebedeff (1987) global using land stations. Brohan et al. (2006) global using land air temperature and sea surface temperature data is the longest of the currently updated global temperature time series (Section 3.2). All time series were smoothed using a 13-point filter. The Brohan et al. (2006) time series are anomalies from 1961 to 1990 mean (°C). Each of the other time series was originally presented as anomalies from the mean temperature of a specific and differing base period. To make them comparable, the other time series have been adjusted to have the mean of their last 30 years identical to that same period in the Brohan et al. (2006) anomaly time series.

Source: IPCC 2007: Physical Science, Figure 1.3

What is regarded by the IPCC as considerably less certain is how much global warming will occur in the future, how fast it will occur, and what impact it will have on the environment and human society. The IPCC argues that the amount and speed of future climate change will depend upon the atmospheric concentrations of greenhouse gases and aerosols, the sensitivity of climate to these changing concentrations, and changes in the internal circulation of the atmosphere and oceans, together with the impact of external influences in the form of variations in solar and volcanic activity.

Computer models, known as general circulation models, or GCMS, are employed by the IPCC to estimate climate outcomes on the basis of a range of assumptions made concerning changes in key social variables such as global population, technological change, energy use, and living standards. The schematic framework underlying these models is shown in Figure 2.2. Here is what the IPCC *Mitigation* report (2007: 182–83) says about the projection of social variables into the future:

> Population is often projected to grow along a pre-described (exogenous) path, while economic activity and emission intensities are projected based on differing assumptions from scenario to scenario. The economic growth path can be based on historical growth rates, convergence assumptions, or on fundamental growth factors, such as saving and investment behaviour, productivity changes, etc. Similarly, future emission intensities can be projected based on historical experience, economic factors, such as labour productivity or other key factors determining structural changes in an economy, or technological development.

Figure 2.2 **Schematic framework representing anthropogenic drivers, impacts of and responses to climate change, and their linkages**

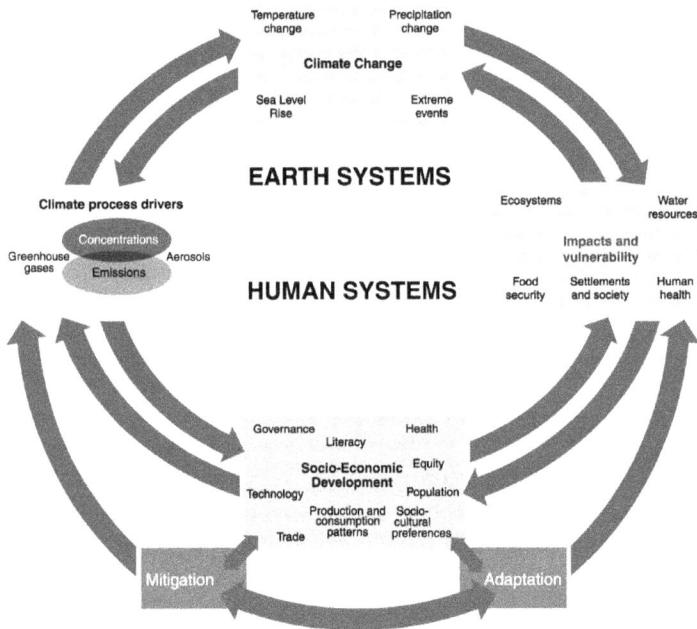

Source: IPCC 2007: Synthesis Report, Figure I.1

These assumptions arise from a range of "scenarios" suggested by the IPCC. While these simulation models are technically sophisticated, they are at heart just simplistic historicist models, in which future outcomes are merely variations on past outcomes. What we think will happen tomorrow is based on what we perceived as happening yesterday. This is hardly a very sophisticated model of the dynamics of human society. Of course, if we are only extrapolating the recent past into the future for just a few years, we won't be too wrong; but if we do this for 100 to 200 years then our extrapolations will inevitably be wildly wrong owing to the power of compound interest and to the probable occurrence of a major structural change in human society. Just compare the world today with how it was around 1800, before the Industrial Revolution had taken hold. We return to this important issue in Chapter 5.

On the basis of these unrealistic simulation models, the IPCC has made the following long-run projections to the year 2100 concerning greenhouse gases and aerosol concentrations:

- Carbon dioxide concentrations will increase in the range of 535 to 983 parts per million (ppm) by 2100 – concentrations 41 to 158 percent higher than current levels (see Figure 2.3).

- Methane concentrations will increase in the range of 1.46 ppm to 3.39 ppm by 2100 – 18 to 91 percent higher.

- Nitrous oxide will increase in the range of 0.36 to 0.46 ppm by 2100 – 11 to 45 percent higher.

More recent work on emissions – the 2008 Garnaut *Draft Report* (ch. 4) – argues that the IPCC calculations are too conservative, and that greenhouse-gas concentrations will increase even more rapidly.

Feeding these emission projections into their computer models of climate change, the IPPC estimates that the Earth's average surface temperature is likely to increase by 1.1°C to 6.4°C by 2100, relative to the base period of 1980 to 1990 (see Figures 2.4 and 2.5). Their best estimate is that temperatures will increase during the twenty-first century in the range 1.8°C to 4.0°C. In other words, it is expected that, on average, the rate of continental warming this century will be at least twice as large – possibly even four times as large – as that in the twentieth century.

Some scientists, however, believe that the IPCC is being too conservative in its warming projections. In a 2005 article in *Nature,* a team of Oxford scientists have suggested that temperatures might even increase in the range 2°C to 11°C. Of course, the higher the rise in temperatures, the greater the cost of any adaptation and mitigation policies.

Figure 2.3 **Carbon dioxide emission projections, 2000–2300**

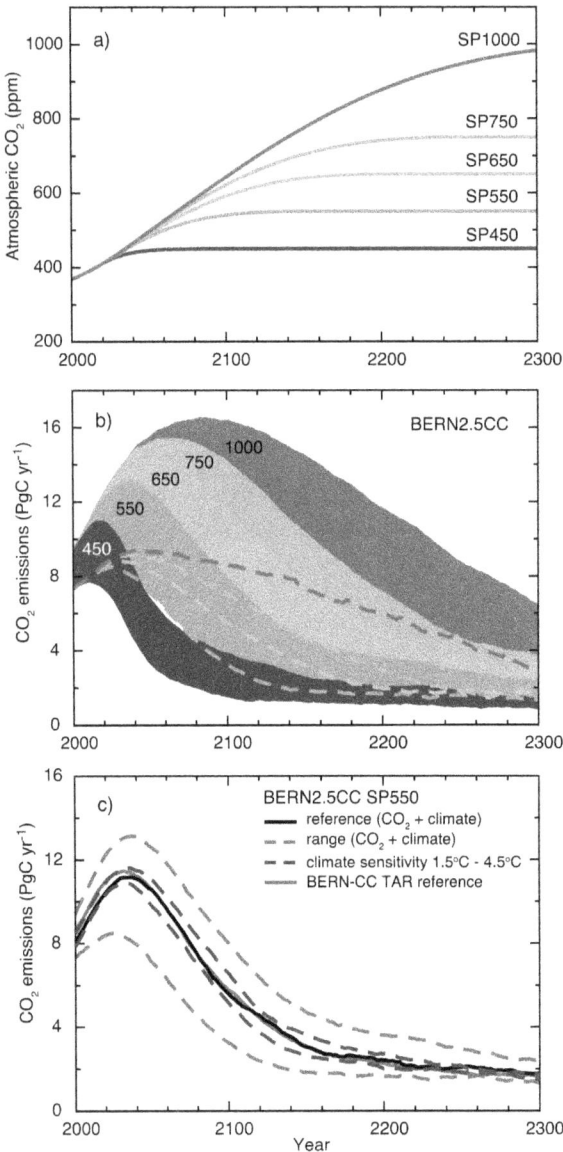

Notes: Project CO_2 emissions leading to stabilization of atmospheric CO_2 concentrations at different levels and the effect of uncertainty in carbon cycle processes on calculated emissions. Panel (a) shows the assumed trajectories of CO_2 concentrations (SP scenarios) (Knutti et al., 2005); (b) and (c) show the implied CO_2 emissions, as projected with the Bern2.5CC EMIC (Joos et al., 2001; Plattner et al., 2001). The ranges given in (b) for each of the SP scenarios represent effects of different model parametrizations and assumptions illustrated for scenario SP550 in panel (c) (range for 'CO_2 + climate'). The upper and lower bounds in (b) are indicated by the top and bottom of the shaded areas. Alternatively, the lower bound (where hidden) is indicated by a dashed line. Panel (c) illustrates emission ranges and sensitivities for scenario SP550.

Source: IPCC 2007: Physical Science, Figure 10.22

Figure 2.4 **Relationship between carbon dioxide concentrations and temperatures, 2000–2100**

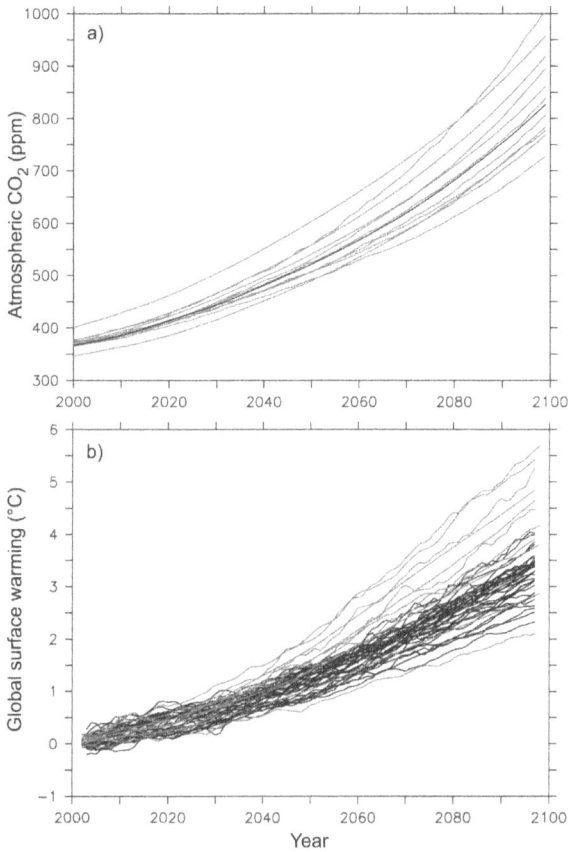

Notes: (a) 21st-century atmospheric CO_2 concentration as simulated by the 11 C⁴MIP models for the SRES A2 emission senario (grey) compared with the standard atmospheric CO_2 concentration used as a forcing for many IPCC AR4 climate models (black). The standard CO_2 concentration values were calculated by the BERN-CC model and are identical to those used in the TAR. For some IPCC-AR4 models, different carbon cycle models were used to convert carbon emissions to atmospheric concentrations. (b) Globally averaged surface temperature change (relative to 2000) simulated by the C⁴MIP models forced by CO_2 emissions (grey) compared to global warming simulated by the IPCC AR4 models forced by CO_2 concentration (black). The C⁴MIP global temperature change has been corrected to account for the non-CO_2 radiative forcing used by the standard IPCC AR4 climate models.

Source: IPCC 2007: Physical Science, Figure 10.20

Figure 2.5 **Past and future temperatures, 1900–2300**

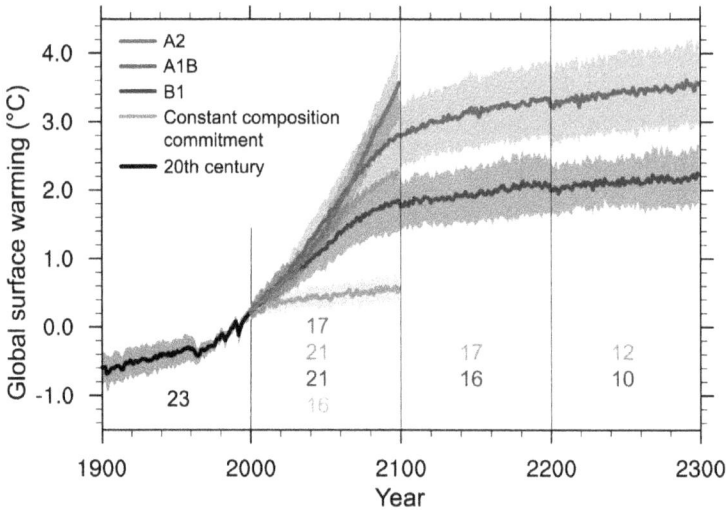

Notes: Multi-model means of surface warming (relative to 1980–1999) for scenarios A2, A1B and B1, shown as continuations of the 20th-century simulation. Values beyond 2100 are for the stabilization scenarios. Linear trends from the corresponding control runs have been removed from these time series. Lines show the multi-model means, shading denotes the ±1 standard deviation range of individual model annual means. Discontinuities between different periods have no physical meaning and are caused by the fact that the number of models that have run a given scenario is different for each period and scenario, as indicated by the grey numbers given for each period and scenario at the bottom of the panel. For the same reason, uncertainly across scenarios should not be interpreted from this figure.

Source: IPCC 2007: Physical Science, Figure 10.4

The anticipated increase in global warming during the twenty-first century is expected to lead to a significant rise in sea levels and to a growing occurrence and intensity of extreme weather events. In its 2007 *Report* the IPCC estimates that the global average sea level will rise by 18 to 59 cm, relative to the 1980 to 1999 level, depending on a range of "scenarios". They argue that sea levels will rise with global warming owing to thermal expansion of ocean water, melting of glaciers and small ice caps, and reduction of the ice sheets of Greenland and Antarctica. But there is considerable uncertainty about some of these sources of sea-level rise. At the moment, scientific understanding of ice-sheet dynamics is insufficient to be able to determine the upper limit for sea-level increases with a high degree of certainty. If, for example, ice flow were to increase in a linear relationship to average global temperature, the upper range of projected sea rise could be 48 to 79 cm by 2100. And if the West Antarctic Ice Sheet were to break up and melt completely, global sea levels would rise by 5 to 6 meters, while the melting of the Greenland ice sheet would raise sea levels by a further 7 meters. The latter two events, however, are, with current knowledge, expected by the IPCC to take centuries and millennia respectively. Once again, the IPCC has taken a conservative approach; and there are some scientists who are willing to speculate that the ice sheets of Greenland and Western Antarctica could disappear by the end of the twenty-first century, adding 12 meters to current sea levels. Clearly this is not good news for the large populations (in the vicinity of hundreds of millions of people) living along coastal margins and in low-lying areas. Of course, as the IPCC fully appreciates, extremist claims will only lead the global community to abandon any attempt to seriously pursue climate mitigation.

Finally, global warming is expected to impact significantly on precipitation and storm intensity. The IPCC expects an increase in the amount and intensity of global precipitation. Climate models suggest that precipitation will increase on average throughout most of northern Europe, northeastern USA, Canada, the Arctic, tropical and eastern Africa, the northern Pacific, and Antarctica, as well as northern Asia and the Tibetan plateau in winter; and that it will decrease on average in most of the Mediterranean, northern Africa, northern Sahara, Central and southwestern America, and the southern Andes, as well as in southwestern Australia during winter. In other words, much of the increase in rainfall will take place over less populated parts of the world, whereas most of the reduction will occur in populated regions. Clearly this will impact on agricultural productivity.

As far as storms are concerned, mid-latitude pathways are projected (by IPCC climate models) to shift towards the poles, with an increased intensity and reduced frequency. Tropical storms are expected to become more intense, to generate stronger peak winds, and to produce greater rainfall. At present the frequency of tropical storms is unclear. The overall impact will be towards greater destruction and the delivery of rainfall less frequently to less productive regions. Once again the global outlook for current forms of agriculture is less favorable. It is recognized, however, that some agricultural regions will initially benefit from modest global warming.

A central theme in the conventional climate-change literature is an emphasis on the possibility of abrupt and unexpected changes in the physical environment – "surprises" as they are often called – as a result of global warming. Some dedicated mitigation engineers like to claim this will be the outcome of passing some hidden threshold level in carbon dioxide (CO_2) – or carbon dioxide equivalent (CO_2e) – some magical "tipping point" as the current fashionistas would have it. The usual suspects rounded up under this rubric include the following three effects. First, a possible breakdown in the current system of oceanic circulation that distributes heat around the globe. In particular, a reversal of the so-called Gulf stream "heat conveyor" would lead to a major cooling of Western Europe and eastern North America, and a corresponding warming of the lower latitudes. This, we are told, will have "disastrous" effects upon existing socioeconomic systems, even though the scientists telling us this are not experts in the responses of human systems.

Second, as mentioned above, some scientists like to speculate that there is a threshold level of CO_2 that will trigger a sudden breakup and melting of the ice sheets of Greenland and Antarctica, which would suddenly raise sea levels by 12 meters, affecting hundreds to thousands of millions of people. Third, unchecked global warming could lead, it is argued, to a sudden outbreak of "runaway carbon dynamics" – a process of rapid increases in carbon dioxide due to the action of positive feedbacks – leading to an acceleration of global warming. This, it is postulated, could occur because of the reversal of land-based carbon sinks in plants and soils, thawing of the permafrost, more frequent fires owing to global warming, and/or the release of methane stored in ice-like hydrate crystals found on the ocean floor. While there is only a small chance of these abrupt changes in physical systems occurring – particularly in some sort of domino sequence – their potentially great impact has caused some scientists to warn of their possible occurrence.

Which is fair enough. But one has the feeling that some enthusiastic mitigation engineers are determined to accumulate as many potential disasters as they can think of in order to improve the acceptance of their arguments. The disaster threshold argument has a particularly long history. It was employed, for example, by the "limits to growth" advocates in the 1970s to 1990s. These ecological engineers made the strong claim that unless economic growth was reduced to zero within a decade, human society would pass the point of no return and self-destruct. Needless to say, it didn't.

At around the same time, James Lovelock (1990), of Gaia fame, made similar claims, and in his latest book *The Revenge of Gaia* (2006) he claims that it is now too late for action, as we have passed the point of no return, and Gaia will punish us for our transgressions against her by eliminating most of our species. Interestingly, Lovelock has always known that a natural crisis would overtake us. In the 1960s he believed, like a large number of other scientists – some (Bryson and Dittberner, 1976) even claiming that carbon dioxide *increases* were *reducing* global temperatures – that it would be the result of the return of a long period of glaciation (a new ice age), which he viewed as the norm for our planet; but now he is convinced it will be a period of global "heating" (a term he prefers to "warming") of our own making. Lovelock has angered many of his own tribe by preaching the virtues of nuclear power and the impotence of the low-carbon technologies beloved of the green movement. One wonders what crisis he (and other natural scientists) might nominate if temperatures decline again over the next few decades as some solar experts are now predicting.

CLIMATE-MITIGATION POLICIES

The growing consensus in the science community is that even without these abrupt "surprises", the modeled rate of global warming in the absence of large-scale corrective action is expected to be much greater than humanity can possibly cope with by adaptive action alone. Accordingly, large-scale government intervention – informed and advised by climate-change experts – in the form of climate mitigation policy is required if the present human and natural systems are to survive. This mitigation policy, we are told by the IPCC, should aim at reducing greenhouse-gas emissions by around 60 to 80 percent by 2100 – some, the zero emission enthusiasts, claim it should be even higher – in order to stabilize atmospheric concentrations of carbon dioxide equivalents in the range 450–55 ppm. Climatic stabilization requires, we are told, that total emissions be limited, some time in the not-too-distant future, to the level removed naturally by the "atmosphere-shallow oceans-land-soil" biota system.

This must be effected, the IPCC insists, by reducing concentrations, by reforestation, and by artificial sequestration through pumping carbon dioxide into the earth and/or deep oceans or by stimulating increased biological activity in shallow oceans. The most technically feasible part of this mitigation program is emission reduction, which scientists believe could be achieved through increased energy efficiency, clean-coal technology, fuel substitution (particularly in motor vehicles), nuclear power, hydropower, solar energy (old not new paradigm), wind power, biomass energy, tidal wave energy, and geothermal energy. All these technologies, it should be noted, are part of the existing industrial technological paradigm rather than the forthcoming technological revolution. The implications will be disused in Chapter 5.

These currently uneconomic low-carbon technologies, which are seen by scientists as the core of the climate-mitigation program, will need to be promoted through government intervention (the favored instrument of the mitigation engineers) in the energy market by imposing either a carbon tax or a "cap and trade" system. This type of action is, of course, the province of the economist rather than the natural scientist and will be discussed further in Chapter 3.

PROBLEMS WITH THE CONVENTIONAL WISDOM

The basic climate-change science appears to be thorough and sound, and I have no intention of challenging it. The detailed analysis of recent changes in global emissions, greenhouse-gas concentrations, temperatures, ice sheet melting, precipitation, and storm activity, together with the role played by humans, has been undertaken by some of the world's most knowledgeable and capable natural scientists.

It should be noted, however, that a number of reputable scientists – such as Dr Ken McCracken, former head of the CSIRO's Division of Space Science, international expert in solar studies, and recipient of the prestigious Australia Prize – who regard themselves as part of the climate-change community, have argued that increased solar output has been responsible for at least part of the global warming detected over the past few decades. McCracken also claims that there will be a reduction in solar activity over the next two decades, which will reduce the impact of human-induced warming, and may even slightly reduce existing temperatures until at least the 2030s; but thereafter temperatures will increase again until the end of the century owing to renewed solar activity, thereby amplifying the impact of human-induced climate change. The climate-change story, therefore, is not as simple as some of the more extreme mitigation engineers would have us believe. And this greater complexity may make it more difficult for them to sell their dreams of large-scale intervention in human society.

While the climate-change science is sound, both the significance attached to recent climate change and the predictions made about future climate change and its likely impact on human society and other living systems are wide of the mark. Even the world's best natural scientists are out of their depth when analyzing the way human systems respond to the physical world. They have no expertise whatsoever in the critically important field of the dynamics of human society.

I will argue, first, that climate-change scientists have drawn the wrong conclusions about the impact of past climate change on human society and, second, that, without a general dynamic theory of human systems, they are incapable of correctly estimating the nature and extent of any future human-induced climate change. In short, the IPCC's estimates of carbon dioxide concentrations throughout the twenty-first century are hopelessly wrong, while those claiming higher concentrations are even more so. Ironically, by insisting that recent climate change is human induced, climate-change scientists have disqualified their entire profession from being taken seriously as expert commentators on *future* climate change. This has opened the door for orthodox economists – an opening they too have failed to negotiate satisfactorily, as shown in Chapter 3.

Drawing the wrong conclusions from history

Consider the conclusions drawn by natural scientists concerning the impact of past climate change on human society. They are quite aware of the existence of abrupt and very rapid climate change during the 150,000-year history of modern man. According to evidence contained in ice cores taken from central Greenland, there have been twenty-four occurrences of abrupt and very rapid periods of climate change in the last 100,000 years. These periods were typically characterized by gradual cooling from a warm interglacial period, followed by more abrupt cooling, then a cold interval and, finally, *an abrupt and rapid warming of around 10°C in only a decade.*

These abrupt and rapid warmings have been called Dansgaard/Oeschger events. The most recent of these is known as the Younger Dryas event, which occurred about 12,800 years ago. This event consisted of a sudden interruption of a gradual warming following the last glaciation. It was a sudden return to a colder climate that lasted for about 1,200 years, and it was followed by a phase of abrupt and very rapid warming of 8°C in a decade, thereby ushering in the type of climate we enjoy today. Hence, the society of modern man has repeatedly experienced a large number of abrupt, rapid, and large-scale climate changes in the period since its first emergence some 150,000 years ago.

What significance have natural scientists drawn from these regular episodes of climate change? Interestingly, these events are either ignored or down-played. For example, attention is diverted from these episodes of climate change by focusing on the undoubted fact that none of them coincided with the phase of civilization in human history. Some argue that while hunter-gatherers were able to successfully negotiate rapid climate change, civilized society – even modern technologically based society – will be unable to do so. The reason, they claim, is that while "prehistoric" societies were small and able to move into more climatically suitable regions, modern societies cannot replicate this response.

This argument neglects a number of critically important matters, which reflects the lack of expertise of natural scientists in the dynamics of human society. One of these matters is that early human societies expanded quite quickly to fully occupy all available land with their given paleolithic technological base. In other words, paleolithic societies fully occupied the globe with their available hunting/gathering technology and, hence, experienced problems similar to those expected of modern societies in the future – namely that there is no unoccupied land for the climatically dispossessed to inhabit. Further, if we temporarily accept the argument that abrupt climate change is dangerous to human society, we would need to acknowledge that Paleolithic societies were more at risk as their populations were small and, in the early years, mankind could have been completely wiped out. Finally, it should be clear that modern technology provides a flexibility of response about which early man could not have even dreamed.

The obvious point, therefore, is that if paleolithic society could prosper and generate the Neolithic Revolution despite experiencing twenty-four episodes of abrupt and very rapid climate change, surely modern man with his mastery over science and technology will be even more successful in this respect. The important implication here is that there is something about the human life-system that enables it to survive and prosper in the face of changes in the natural environment and in climate. But, by dismissing the experience of Paleolithic societies and by focusing exclusively on the last 10,000 years, natural scientists are able to pretend that the severity of the current episode of climate change is unprecedented and uniquely dangerous.

During the past 10,000 years there have been, of course, considerable fluctuations in climate, albeit not of the same magnitude as in earlier times. In Europe, for example, a warm period occurred between 1000 and 1270 AD, followed by the Little Ice Age from 1270 to 1850. These changes in climate would have influenced the pattern of economic activities but they had no significant impact on the transformation of a relatively backward part of the world into the global industrial powerhouse it had become by the middle of the nineteenth century. I have analyzed this transition, using my dynamic-strategy theory in *The Ephemeral Civilization* (1997). This analysis also exposes the fatal flaws in the attempts by some environmentalists to explain the rise and fall of societies in terms of changes in climate.

The climate mitigationists only draw attention to earlier episodes of climate change to make the point that the present fairly stable situation could easily be transformed suddenly into one that is totally out of control. One prominent climate-change scientist – Barry Pittock in *Climate Change* (2006: 40) – claims:

> Despite only gradual changes in driving forces, these observed rapid climate changes [in the past] appear to have occurred because the drivers reached some sort of tipping point or threshold at which climate flips into a new state. Such mechanisms suggest that similar rapid climate changes could happen again, even when driven by only gradual increases in greenhouse gases.

The concept of "tipping points" or "critical thresholds" – which are not explored either theoretically or empirically – is employed by Pittock and others to fill the void left by the absence of a satisfactory general dynamic theory of climate change. It is all a matter of intellectual smoke and mirrors, which has no scientific basis.

The real lesson to be derived from the pattern of repeated abrupt and rapid climate change during the history of modern humans has been totally ignored by natural scientists. The real lesson is that *the human life-system*, which enables us to survive and prosper in a hostile world, *has been shaped in part by the regular occurrence of abrupt and rapid climate change*. Modern man, in other words, is part of a dynamic life-system that is able not only to survive climate change, but also to prosper in the face of its fiercest onslaughts. As I have shown elsewhere (Snooks, 1996; 1997; 1998a; 2003), the human life-system has been able to grow at an exponential rate – as described by the Snooks-Panov algorithm – over the past 150,000 years, despite living in a hostile environment. In effect, the dynamic process of human society has not missed a beat throughout this long period of time. This is the lesson that natural scientists have ignored – the good news that the mitigation engineers don't want to hear. In Chapter 5 I show that there are good theoretical and empirical reasons for concluding that our dynamic life-system will enable us to continue to survive and prosper in the face of the current climate-change event.

Employing the wrong models

Consider the range of carbon dioxide concentrations and temperatures projected by the IPCC's models. While not wanting to challenge the climate science about the relationship between fossil-fuel emissions and global temperatures, I totally reject the models used to estimate future emissions. Once again the problem faced by the IPCC is their failure to construct a realist general dynamic theory of human society. Because of this failure, they are unable to model the technological development path of human society, and have totally overlooked the forthcoming technological paradigm shift – the fourth economic revolution in human history. Instead they employ naive historicist models that merely extrapolate into the future key economic variables (population, living standards, energy use, etc.) on a range of different, but inadequate, assumptions based on recent experience. As shown in Chapter 5, my dynamic-strategy theory – a realist general dynamic theory – is able to model the underlying exponential technological development path and, thereby, is able to predict the next technological revolution – the real Solar Revolution – beginning in the middle decades of this century. This major discovery renders all IPCC emission scenarios and estimates – together with the temperature estimates based on them – totally redundant. Accordingly, the recent lobbying of governments by natural scientists on the issue of climate mitigation is no more than empty posturing, as they just don't possess the necessary expertise. Before outlining the new science of societal dynamics – the only valid basis for government policy concerning future climate change – we need to see what contribution orthodox economics has made to the climate-change debate.

Chapter 3
The Limitations of Orthodox Economics

The door leading economists into the climate-change debate was opened by natural scientists insisting that recent climate change is human induced. As orthodox, or neoclassical, economics is largely based on the microeconomic analysis of prices and the costs and benefits of investment expenditures, it was inevitable that its practitioners would attempt to economically evaluate alternative policies of climate mitigation. The question tackled in this chapter is: What are the costs and benefits of the contribution of orthodox economics to the climate-change debate? And the answer is that the costs greatly, dangerously, exceed the benefits.

THE ECONOMICS OF CLIMATE CHANGE

Because the current phase of climate change is said to be human induced, orthodox economists have been able to hijack the policy debate, leaving natural scientists out in the cold. Neoclassical economists believe they have the rational answer to every policy decision involving resources, expenditures, prices, taxes and profits, no matter how large the problem or how long its duration. As one of the major participants in the policy debate, Nicholas Stern, author of the recent *Stern Review* (2007: 319) on the economics of climate change, has written:

> Science reveals the nature of the danger and provides the foundations for the technologies that can enable the world to avoid them. Economics offers a framework that can help policymakers decide how much action to take and with what policy instruments. It can also help people understand the issues and form views about both the appropriate behaviour and policies. The scientific and economic framework provides a structure for the discussions necessary to get to grips with the global challenge and guidance in setting rational and consistent national and international policies.

While most orthodox economists believe they have the theoretical tools and statistical techniques to engage successfully with the central issues and policies concerning climate, it is the development economists who feel most comfortable advocating the massive degree of government intervention involved in climate mitigation. Why? Because development economists have become accustomed to urging large-scale government intervention in the less-developed world to promote economic development. And they have become experts in justifying large-scale intervention on the grounds of both "market failure" and "ethics". As the subtitle of one his recent books suggests, Nicholas Stern's (2005) concern is with "Making Development Happen", presumably because he believes it cannot happen without him and his colleagues. Even though economic development is as old as human society, the "development industry" has existed only since the mid-twentieth century: and yet development economists like Nicholas Stern believe that their discipline is essential to the economic rise of the lesser-developed world! This argument is presented more fully in my book *Global Transition* (Snooks 1999).

It is not a very large step for these professional interventionists to take from the arena of economic development to that of climate mitigation – from the lesser-developed world to the entire global community. Not all economists, however, feel comfortable with the degree of intervention being advocated by the mitigation engineers. Many economists believe in the sanctity of free markets and need to be convinced that a market has failed systematically before they are willing to sanction large-scale government intervention. This is why mitigation engineers like Nicholas Stern place so much emphasis on "market failure".

IS ECONOMICS UP TO THE TASK?

Orthodox economists are completely confident that their theory of capitalist production is more than capable of analyzing all societal issues. I will argue, however, that the ability of neoclassical economics to analyze reality is severely limited. How confident can we be in a science that employs as its model of human society the hypothetical "firm"?

The nature of modern economics

Neoclassical economics emerged from the "marginal revolution" of the 1870s, which was pioneered by W.S. Jevons (1835–1882) in England, Carl Menger (1840–1921) in Austria, and Léon Walras (1834–1910) in Lausanne. This mathematically based "theory of value" or "theory of the firm", which was elegantly summarized by Alfred Marshall (1842–1924), is concerned with small (or marginal) changes in markets in the short-term within a comparative static (rather than a dynamic) framework. The theory of the firm, which is preoccupied with conditions of equilibrium (rather than the disequilibrium of dynamics), reflects the nineteenth-century influence of classical thermodynamics. This mechanical physics-like approach to human society displaced the earlier, more organic science of classical economics – pioneered by the French Physiocrats and Adam Smith (1723–1790) in the eighteenth century, and Karl Marx (1818-1883) in the nineteenth century – which focused on longer-run dynamic processes underlying the transformation of human society. These issues are discussed in greater detail in my book *Economics Without Time* (1993). Since the late nineteenth century, orthodox economics has been largely concerned with everyday economic issues examined within a short-run, static framework. As the Cambridge Post-Keynesian economist Joan Robinson famously said, neoclassical economics is trivially concerned with "the price of a cup of tea".

The theoretical tools that orthodox economists bring to the table when discussing climate change – anything but a trivial or static issue – include: cost–benefit analysis, price theory, the shadowy theory of external diseconomies (somewhat loosely called "externalities"), and market failure. These somewhat meager tools of microeconomics are expected to handle the big macro issues of the dynamics of human society and its interaction with climate change throughout the next century or so. This is like turning up to the gunfight at OK Corral with a Swiss Army knife – a very effective tool for small jobs but completely outgunned in the world of realist dynamics.

It is hardly surprising that neoclassical economics has failed to develop a realist theory of dynamics. Its misnamed "growth theory" is not growth theory at all, as it focuses merely on convergence to equilibrium in the tradition of classical thermodynamics mentioned above. Economics failed to follow the lead of physics in the twentieth century when a reformulated thermodynamics shifted its focus to far-from-equilibrium conditions. As neoclassical growth theory has little to say about real-world dynamics, it is not even invoked by climate-change economists.

To his credit, Nicholas Stern is aware of some of the deficiencies in neoclassical economics. As a development economist he certainly should be. He tells us, for example, that:

> Standard externality and cost-benefit approaches have their usefulness for analysing climate change, but, as they are methods focused on evaluating marginal changes, and generally abstract from dynamics and risk, they can only be starting points for further work …

> Standard treatments of discounting are valuable for analysing marginal projects but are inappropriate for non-marginal comparisons of [development] paths; the approach to discounting must meet the challenge of assessing and comparing paths that have very different trajectories and involve very long-term and large inter-generational impacts. (Stern 2007: 25)

But, as an orthodox economist, Stern's dilemma is that he has no other theoretical instruments to substitute for these static, short-term, marginal concepts. So, despite his qualifications, Stern is forced to resort to these inadequate theoretical instruments anyway. And by employing totally inappropriate tools of analysis, Stern and the rest of his tribe have contributed to "the great climate-mitigation delusion". As the mitigation engineers have failed to understand the dynamics of human society, they are unable to analyze the future either of human society or the planet. It is like placing a teashop proprietor in charge of the future of humanity.

Unfortunately most orthodox economists are just not aware of the full extent of the limitations of their profession. Why? Because these theoretically trained economists rarely encounter big issues in the real world; and, if they do, they skate across the deficiencies of their methods with heroic boldness. Whenever static costs exceed static benefits, which is often the case with big real-world issues, orthodox economists usually suggest that the participants must be economically irrational, or driven by non-material motivations.

The failure of economics to explain reality

The deficiencies of neoclassical economics are glaringly obvious when applied to big historical events, as has been done quite innocently by the so-called New Economic Historians – neoclassical economists who turned their attention to history, particularly in the USA from the 1960s. A few examples – including US railroads, the American War of Independence, the US Civil War, and the economic pay-off of the British empire – will help to illustrate my argument about the limited ability of economics when examining big, real-world issues. In order not to obscure our main argument, these historical examples will be dealt with briefly. Interested readers may wish to consult my other books where they are developed in more detail.

In the celebrated case of the economic role of US railroads, the historical economist Robert Fogel (1964) employed neoclassical theory to measure the static costs and benefits of American investment in transport technology. He estimated the "social saving" from railroad investment to have been only about 4 percent of GNP in 1890 (which was much less than other economic activities) and concluded, therefore, that railroads played only a limited role in American economic development. According to Fogel – later jointly (with Douglass North) awarded the Nobel Prize in Economics for his promotion of neoclassical theory in history – railroads were not essential to American growth in the second half of the nineteenth century, and that their role could have been performed largely by existing river and canal systems. What his neoclassical analysis completely overlooks are the dynamic benefits of creating, in response to strategic demand, an integrated mega-market in the second half of the nineteenth century that was to facilitate the unfolding of the USA's technological strategy – an unfolding process that enabled the USA to achieve world economic dominance in the twentieth century. As I show in *The Ephemeral Civilization* (1997: 374–76), railway construction was not economically marginal but rather was central to this development.

In the case of the American War of Independence, neoclassically inspired economic historians have attempted to measure the static costs and benefits to the American colonialists of British imperialism. To do this they have estimated the annual costs of "distortions of trade routes" resulting from the Navigation Acts imposed by Britain between 1763 and 1775. Traditionally, these costs, which have been regarded as the main burden of empire, amounted to no more than 3 percent of gross colonial product. As such they would have been largely offset by benefits from being part of the British empire, which included British subsidies, bounties, and military protection. Others have argued that the costs of taxes and customs imposed by Britain after the war with France, together with the restrictions resulting from the 1763 Proclamation Line (defining the western boundary of the colonies) were not terribly onerous. The conclusion? That politics rather than economics explains the very costly and risky fight by the Americans for independence, when they had so little to gain economically. It was a long and costly war that was only won after French involvement. Yet why would the Americans risk so much for political ends? The real answer is that the neoclassical evaluation of the static costs of empire do not come close to approximating the dynamic costs. As we shall see in Chapter 5, the same is true of the static costs of climate mitigation. The struggle for independence was a fight for control of very different dynamic strategies. The British were pursuing a global commerce strategy and wanted, as a maritime power, to confine American settlement to the eastern seaboard; whereas the colonialists were pursing the family-multiplication strategy and wanted, as a potential continental power, to expand westward. It was a clash of dynamic strategies, and the costs of being dominated by the British can be measured in terms of the huge potential gains that could be made by forging a mega-market across North America. To convert these potential costs into realized benefits was why the Americans were prepared to risk so much. There are, of course, lessons to be learnt here for the potential clash in the twenty-first century between the antistrategic mitigation engineers and the global strategists. It could become a clash of dynamic strategies on a far more massive scale than that of the War of Independence. And it would be far more costly.

When considering the static costs and benefits of the American Civil War (1861–1865), Robert Fogel (1989) is led by his neoclassical training to argue that as the cost of this internecine conflict – including the deaths of 600,000 men and the destruction of much infrastructure – outweighed the apparent benefits, the war must have been fought over the moral issue of slavery. This is a very odd conclusion, as my study of human history suggests that men in massive numbers do not surrendor their lives for moral issues. And, in fact, when we take the dynamic benefits into account, as in *The Ephemeral Civilization* (1997: 378–84), it is clear that the US Civil War was a clash between two very different dynamic strategies. The North was desperate to maintain the political integrity of the USA in order to develop a mega-market under tariff protection, which would drive its burgeoning technological strategy based on its industrial facilities in the north-east. In contrast, the South was equally desperate to achieve independence from the protectionist North in order to pursue its free-trade commerce strategy based on the export of plantation crops, particularly cotton, to Britain in exchange for cheap industrial products. The potential dynamic benefits to both camps arising from the success of their strategic goals were huge, and greatly in excess of the high costs of this long, drawn-out, and expensive war. The victory of the North led to the transformation of the USA into the world's largest and most prosperous society in the twentieth century, although at the cost of a depressed South. This global dominance would not have occurred in a politically and, hence, economically fragmented North America.

Finally, consider the economic basis for the British empire after 1885. Some have argued – as outlined in *The Ephemeral Civilization* (Snooks 1997: 292–

300) – that after 1885, the return on investment in empire was significantly lower than that at home or abroad; that the real beneficiaries of empire were the colonials/dominionists; that those in the UK who benefited most were the aristocrats at the expense of the tax-paying middle classes; and that between 1870 and 1913, the static gains were only 1 to 6 percent of GNP, compared with 10 percent on railways. Hence, the post-1885 empire is seen by neoclassically inspired historians as economically irrational and anachronistic. Once again, however, the dynamic benefits have been ignored. The major dynamic benefit of empire, which accrued to UK's tax-paying middle classes, was the role it played in *defending* and enhancing Britain's dynamic strategy of technological change, which generated high rates of continuous economic growth. Empire guaranteed Britain's post-1885 survival and security. I argue that empire was only abandoned when Britain found a more economical method of defending its technological strategy at home – the atomic bomb. As soon as the bomb was developed, Britain dismantled its empire and emerged richer than ever.

In all these historical case studies, the costs are easily measured in a static framework, but not so the most important benefits that are always dynamic in nature. As we will see in detail in Chapter 5, the same is true when neoclassical economics is applied to climate change. As always, the dynamic benefits of the strategic pursuit are completely neglected. Also neoclassical economists fail to understand the mutual destruction that always arises from the clash of opposing dynamic strategies. The bottom line is that orthodox economics is a totally unsuitable discipline for dealing with the big dynamic issues in human society – particularly the big issue of climate change.

WHAT ABOUT THE MODELS EMPLOYED?

Because orthodox economics has failed to construct a general dynamic theory of human society, it is forced to fall back on naive historicist models when estimating the impact of either climate change or proposed mitigation policies. There is a major irony here. Orthodox economists pride themselves on their superior deductive approach to constructing economic theory and are largely contemptuous of the work of historical economists who employ inductive techniques. While they continue to focus on problems of "the-price-of-a-cup-of-tea" variety – of short-term, static and marginal (trivial) issues — they can maintain their self-delusion. But when they take on long-term, dynamic, and non-marginal (important) issues they find themselves completely out of their depth. Of course, it usually takes someone else to point it out.

If neoclassical economists insist on exploring the big issues like climate change, their only option – like that of the IPCC – is to employ the historicist models that historical economists reject as being simplistic and, therefore, dangerous. These historicist models involve extrapolating key economic variables into the future on the basis of a range of arbitrary assumptions. The technical sophistication of these models – which may seem impressive to the uninitiated – doesn't alter the fact that they fail to capture the dynamics of human society. They have, in other words, no way of taking into account any major structural changes that might occur as a result of the internal dynamics of human society. Ironically, only the inductively based theory of the historical economist is able to achieve this essential requirement.

The historicist models employed in the *Stern Report* are called "integrated assessment models" (or IAMs). These IAMs include a range of sectors, such as agriculture, forestry, fisheries, water systems, energy supplies, ecosystems, coastal zones and so on. Stern (2007: 164) claims that: "IAMs simulate the process of human-induced climate change, from emissions of GHGs [greenhouse gases] to the socio-economic impacts of climate change". The modeled chain of impacts – which also includes feedback effects – operates from population, technology, production and consumption to emissions to atmospheric concentrations to "radiative forcing" and global climate to regional climate and weather to direct impacts (crops, forests and ecosystems) to socioeconomic impacts.

The IAMs are employed to make calculations of impacts on climate, environment, and human society *for periods of up to 200 years into the future*. All without considering the probability of major structural change over this long period of time. Of course, if we go 200 years or so back into the past, we enter a very different (pre-industrial) world to that existing today. Imagine the impact that the structural change called the Industrial Revolution would have had on the credibility of any historicist models (using similarly unrealistic or ephemeral assumptions) that might have been estimated in the late eighteenth century for the following 200 years! It does not seem to have occurred to the neoclassical authors of these models that their projections will be just as wildly inaccurate.

WHAT IS THE ECONOMISTS' STORY?

It is a simple story. Using the textbook theory of the firm, the *Stern Report* attempts to calculate the costs of "business as usual" pursued in the face of hypothetical climate change over the next **two** centuries, compared with the costs of "stabilizing" climate change (by preventing any further increase in greenhouse-gas concentrations) over the same time period. Of course, they employ estimates of emissions, concentrations, and temperature change generated by their unrealistic historicist IAMs. Stern (2007: xv) summarizes his simple analysis and calculations as follows:

> Using the results from formal economic models, the Review estimates that if we don't act, the overall costs and risk of climate change will be equivalent to losing at least 5% of global GDP each year now and forever. If a wider range of risks and impacts is taken into account, the estimates of damage could rise to 20% of GDP or more.

> In contrast, the costs of action – reducing greenhouse emissions to avoid the worst impacts of climate change – can be limited to around 1% of global GDP each year.

On the basis of these simple calculations, the rational course of action, according to the orthodox economist seems clear: a climate-mitigation program will, in the long run, be less costly than "business as usual". The cost of mitigation is portrayed as being quite modest and manageable – merely 1% of GDP or $1 in every $100 we produce. A reasonable insurance policy? Actually it is not quite as reasonable as it looks, as it is about ten times the rate we would expect to pay on our house insurance, but I suppose a habitable planet is more important to us than our individual houses.

Actually, the scale of the intervention being proposed through climate mitigation can only be fully appreciated by looking at it in absolute terms. One percent of world GDP, which currently (2007) amounts to $656.1 billion, is a very large figure – more than the USA spends on its military program (about $560 billion) each year. And this would be required in each and every year forever. Another way of looking at this matter is to estimate the amount of cumulative investment and employment that would be required by 2050 in low-carbon technologies as part of this mitigation program. Stern (2007: 304) tells us that the cumulative investment required will amount to US$13 trillion – that is 13 followed by twelve zeros! – and the number of workers required would be 25 million – more than the entire population of Australia. *Clearly, this is intervention on a massive scale.*

THE JUSTIFICATION FOR MASSIVE INTERVENTION

Intervention on this global scale is difficult for neoclassical economists to justify. The theory of the firm is based on the key idea that the best – that is the most efficient – outcomes are experienced when markets are allowed to operate with minimal interference. The only way neoclassical economists can rationalize significant intervention is when the market system has failed. Normally, "market failure" is invoked to justify *occasional* small-scale interventions, otherwise intervention, rather than freely operating markets, becomes the rule rather than the exception. Which makes nonsense of a market-based economics. A major market imperfection is what economists call external diseconomies (referred to rather loosely by Stern as "externalities"), which arise when the action of one producer causes costs for other producers – costs that the offending producer does not have to bear himself – such as downstream pollution of water or air. It should be realized that the concept of external economies is a shadowy one, particularly when it is extended from producers to the entire global society. Tibor Scitovsky (1954), one of the pioneers of this economic concept, wrote: "The concept of external economies is one of the most illusive in economic literature". As I show later, it is also an artificial concept that owes its existence to the myopic focus of neoclassical economics on a small subset – the producer – of the wider human life-system.

Because of the massive scale of intervention required to stabilize greenhouse-gas concentrations, climate-change economists go into overdrive concerning "market failure", "market imperfections", "barriers" to "sustainable" and "ethical" outcomes, and to "externalities". Stern, for example, is able to detect market imperfections in every nook and cranny (or should that be every crook and nanny?) in the global economy. He tells us, for example:

> In common with many other environmental problems, human-induced climate change is at its most basic level an externality. Those who produce greenhouse-gas emissions are bringing about climate change, thereby imposing costs on the world and on future generations, but they do not face directly, neither via markets nor in other ways, the full consequences of the costs of their actions ... so they face little or no economic incentive to reduce emissions. Similarly, emitters do not have to compensate those who lose out because of climate change. In this sense, human-induced climate change is an externality, one that is not 'corrected' through any institution or market, unless policy intervenes ... All in all, it [climate change] must be regarded as market failure on the greatest scale the world has seen. (Stern 2007: 27)

In addition to the idea that climate change is market failure "on the greatest scale the world has seen", Sterns finds "barriers" to rational behavior and motivation together with "market imperfections" *everywhere* in modern society. To his mind this justifies not only a carbon tax that will force carbon emitters to mend their ways, but also a whole network of government interventions in the form of support for uncompetitive low-carbon technologies, regulations, information disclosure, and "persuasion", as well as direct investment by the public sector in energy conservation.

THE GOALS AND INSTRUMENTS OF INTERVENTION

The mitigation engineers believe, therefore, that owing to systemic market failure, even in the most progressive societies, it is the responsibility of governments, advised by right-minded experts, to establish the goals, incentives and rules to save us from ourselves. The private sector's role in this agenda is to respond passively to the directions of the mitigation engineers rather than creatively to the requirements of the dynamic process underlying their life-system. What the mitigation engineers are proposing is the establishment of a series of command economies at both the national and international levels. In this section we will review the way in which this is to be done.

The *Stern Review* advocates a tripartite mitigation policy to stabilize greenhouse gas concentrations in the range 450–550 ppm in carbon dioxide equivalents (CO_2e). First, it is necessary, we are told, to establish an "appropriate" price for carbon through government imposition of taxes, trading, or regulation. While this will redirect the costs of climate change back to the carbon producers, thereby providing them with "incentives" to modify their activities, this manipulation of energy prices will not be sufficient. Stern is adamant that owing to "a range of other market failures and barriers ... carbon pricing alone is not sufficient". Secondly, therefore, he and his colleagues claim that "technology policy ... is vital to bring forward the range of low-carbon and high efficiency technologies that will be needed to make deep emissions cuts". This will involve R&D, demonstration, and market-support policies to "help *drive* innovation, and *motivate* a response by the private sector". Thirdly, Stern insists that "policies to remove the barriers to *behavioural* change ... policies on regulation, information and financing ... and a *shared understanding* of the nature of climate change and its consequences, should be fostered through evidence, *education, persuasion and discussion*" (Stern 2007: 349; my emphasis).

Hence, it is not enough for governments to restructure the ordinary market mechanism. It is also considered necessary to "drive" innovation, "motivate" strategists, and to change the thinking and behavior of all citizens through "education" and "persuasion". Can there be any doubt that the mitigation engineers want to transform our free-enterprise societies into command societies in which they set the goals and ensure they are achieved by a very wide range of instruments of intervention? All in the name of saving us from ourselves. What, one wonders, will be necessary in the world envisaged by the mitigation engineers if and when the measures of government "education and persuasion" fail? Coercion?

Of particular interest here is Stern's view of market intervention and control. He calls it "harnessing markets for mitigation" – riding markets like horses! The theory used to justify this unprecedented degree of intervention in democratic societies is textbook short-run, static price theory, showing the likely impact of taxes on prices and output – theory concerning "the price of a cup of tea". To his credit, Stern is aware of some of the limitations involved in employing a short-term policy framework to deal with long-term issues of global significance. "The challenge", he writes, "is how to ensure that the short-term policy framework remains on track to deliver the long-term stabilisation goal" (Stern 2007: 359). His response to this challenge is to argue that policy instruments – such as a carbon tax – should be employed in a flexible way to continually keep society in the vicinity of its "stabilisation target". Stern (2007: 360) tells us:

> The stabilisation target is analogous to the inflation target. In the UK, the Monetary Policy Committee each month sets a short-term policy instrument, the interest rate on central bank money, until their next meeting, in order to keep inflation on track to hit its target. The analogy with climate-change policy would be the setting of a tax rate or an emissions trading quote for, say, a five year period, with firms and households making their own decisions about emissions reductions subject to that carbon-price path and their expectations about policy-makers' committment to the long-term stabilisation goal.

This is fascinating. Stern actually links stabilization targeting with inflation targeting! Fascinating because for the past decade or so, I have been making the point that inflation targeting is a policy instrument that is damaging the dynamic mechanism of the human life-system, which will have a detrimental impact on our material progress (Snooks 1997b; 1998b; 2008b; 2008c). That damage is now (late 2008-early 2009) evident in the emerging global problems of slower (even negative) growth and increasing unemployment. If an analogy is to be drawn from inflation targeting, it is that stabilization targeting will also inflict damage on the underlying dynamic mechanism, albeit in a different way. This is discussed below.

But stabilization targeting is, according to the *Stern Review*, not sufficient, even in developed countries, to motivate business people and consumers to meet their mitigation goal. The reason, as usual, is that capitalist society is riddled with market failure. It is necessary, therefore, to employ a wide variety of additional instruments of intervention in order to transform our industrial society into a low-carbon society.

The first barrage of instruments of intervention are necessary, Stern tells us, to accelerate the adoption of low-carbon technologies that otherwise would remain uncompetitive. These are referred to as "deployment policies". Stern (2007: 421) claims that "deployment policies encourage the private sector to develop and deploy low-carbon technologies". The deployment policies are wide-ranging and include fiscal incentives, capital grants, "feed-in" tariffs, quotas, subsidies and skewed procurement policies by public monopolies and local and national governments. In other words: "protection all round". Governments are also encouraged to fine-tune their intellectual property regimes and to judiciously employ planning and licensing regulations to smooth the path for companies employing low-carbon technologies.

But even this degree of intervention is insufficient to implement the goals of the mitigation engineers. Stern (2007: 427) explains:

> Policies to price greenhouse gas, and support technology development, are fundamental to tackle climate change. However, *even if these measures are taken, barriers and market imperfections may still inhibit action, particularly on energy efficiency*. These barriers and failures include hidden and *transaction costs* such as the cost of the time needed to plan new investments; *lack of information* about available options; capital constraints; misaligned incentives; as well as *behavioural and organisational factors* affecting economic rationality in decision-making. These market imperfections result in *significant obstacles to the uptake* of cost-effective mitigation, and weakened drivers for innovation, particularly in markets for *energy efficiency* measures.

Owing to all these alleged market failures and barriers, it is remarkable that human society has been able to get along without the mitigation engineers for so long – like 150,000 years.

The policy instruments suggested by the *Stern Review* to overcome these anticipated problems fall into the categories of regulation, information, and finance. Regulation, they believe, is required to communicate policy intentions; reduce uncertainty, complexity, and transaction costs; induce innovation; and, ironically, to avoid technological "lock-in". This regulation, as I show in chapter 5, will actually contribute to locking the global economy into the old exhausted technological paradigm. Information policies on the other hand, are required to disseminate best-practice ideas, and to "help consumers and firms make sounder decisions and stimulate more competitive markets for more energy efficient goods and services". And financing policy should encourage private investment to raise energy efficiency, while direct government investment should focus on energy conservation. These suggestions, of course, are based on the very shaky assumption that the mitigation experts and their compliant government bureaucracies are better placed than consumers and "strategists" (or economic decision-makers) to understand where the best interests of human society lie.

It is certainly clear from this very comprehensive network of instruments of intervention that Stern and his fellow mitigation engineers are encouraging governments to assume responsibility for the direction to be taken by human society in the future. While they claim that the response to centrally determined goals, incentives, regulations and directives is the responsibility of the private sector, it is also clear that it has been cast in a minor and passive role. The major and active role is to be played by governments, bureaucracies, and their climate-change advisors.

The proposed global climate-mitigation program is a major and unprecedented experiment in reshaping and redirecting human society on both a national and international scale. In modern history, the closest approach to this type of societal experiment was the command economy of the USSR in the twentieth century. Both the "mitigation economy" and the USSR had their goals set not by strategists but by interventionist metaphysicians (by environmentalists or by Marxists, who are moved by faith rather than reality); both the mitigation economy and the USSR established a comprehensive network of metaphysically determined prices, rules, regulations, incentives, and technologies to manipulate consumer demand and to constrain the activities of firms (or "enterprises"). The main difference between these two heavily regulated systems are the greater freedom of prices and decision makers in the mitigation economy, which in economic terms is the least significant issue.

If you are able to centrally determine the goals and broad network of incentives, rules, regulations and technologies, you are able to take control of an economic system away from the strategists and place it in the hands of the interventionist metaphysicians. By doing so you turn a strategic society into an antistrategic society – a free enterprise economy into a command economy. Only strategic societies survive and prosper in the longer term because only strategists with a high degree of responsibility and freedom of action are able to respond, via strategic demand, to the requirements of their life-system. The interventionists respond instead to misleading metaphysical ideas, such as Marxism, neo-liberalism (inflation targeting), or radical environmentalism.

The proof of this argument can be found in the collapse of the USSR – a society hijacked by metaphysical interventionists – after only three generations. Goals, incentives and technologies must be established by freely operating markets if human society is to survive and prosper – they must be established according to strategic values and not metaphysical values.

Interventionists fail not only in the big things, such as creating command economies like the USSR, but also in smaller things, like the various attempts to "fix" the so-called "global financial crisis" of the last quarter of 2008. Governments around the world, advised by metaphysical interventionists, attempted to rescue their financial institutions by injections of large quantities of tax-payers' money, and by giving grandiose guarantees of total protection to bank deposits. The latter "solution" was chosen by the Australian Rudd government, despite the fact that the Australian banking system, in contrast to sections of that in the USA, was regarded as very sound at that time. The immediate and very predictable response by the public, was a major run on non-bank deposits held by financial institutions not covered by these guarantees, followed by the equally predictable reaction by affected financial institutions in freezing billions of dollars of these deposits. This led to a major, if temporary, distortion of markets and much personal distress. Hence, because the Australian government, and its economic advisors, had no understanding of the dynamics of their economy, instability was injected into an otherwise secure system. Similarly, the large-scale injection of funds into failing financial institutions around the world will distort the market mechanism of the dynamic life-system. Imagine, therefore, the economic problems that will be created by the massive intervention required to implement a serious climate mitigation program.

Another recent classical example of an intervention that misfired is the attempt by the USA after September Eleven to secure oil supplies (rather than the stated aim of eliminating "weapons of mass destruction") in the Middle East by invading Iraq and deposing Saddam Hussein. The problem seemed simple and tractable. Certainly for a superpower it was a simple matter to destroy the conventional military forces in Iraq and to eliminate the antistrategic leadership of the Hussein family and the Bathist Party (yet more difficult to find the nonexistent weapons of mass destruction), but it proved to be impossible to predict the shape and longer-term outcomes of intervention in a complex sociopolitical system. All the USA has so far (late 2008) achieved is to destroy the old Iraqi dynamic life-system and fail to replace it with a more satisfactory one. Iraqi society is now totally dysfunctional. The Bush administration had no conception of the complexity of what they were attempting, and their "expert" advisors had no understanding of the existence or operation of the dynamic life-system. The military intervention predictably failed to achieve the original objective, and was instrumental in the removal of the Republicans from the White House. Failed interventions by democratic governments always result in prompt political change.

The issue of who sets the goals and incentives transcends the usual discussion of the relative efficiency of the public and private sectors. But even at this level, Stern and his fellow mitigation engineers are hopelessly optimistic. They believe that government ministers and bureaucrats – guided by the mitigation "experts" – can improve the efficiency of the private sector. This, however, is clearly not the case, primarily because public servants are not directly exposed to the consequences of their decisions and actions in the way business people are. We are all familiar with the poor quality of real-world decision making of public servants in regulating the private sector and in operating government monopolies. It is unrealistic to expect public servants to devise and sustain efficient energy and production systems through the indirect means at their disposal, and totally bizarre to expect them to devise and sustain our dynamic life-system.

THE COSTS AND BENEFITS OF ECONOMICS

Owing to the failure of orthodox economics to develop a general dynamic theory of human society – a subject in which they have displayed not the slightest interest over the past 150 years – its story about climate mitigation and the future of humanity is not only pure fiction, it is also highly misleading and dangerous. While admitting their theoretical tools have certain limitations, orthodox economists have not told the complete truth. The complete truth is that while they have something to say about small, short-term issues that can be handled in a static framework, they have nothing to say about big, long-term issues that can only be dealt with dynamically. While they can isolate forces determining "the price of a cup of tea", orthodox economists are unable to model the underlying dynamic forces that will determine the changing nature not only of civilization but also of the Earth's climate as the twenty-first century unfolds.

By analyzing the costs and benefits of a proposed comprehensive mitigation program in a static rather than a dynamic framework, orthodox economists have provided an entirely false picture about the possible futures facing us. As I show in Chapter 5, by ignoring the dynamic costs of climate mitigation, these keepers of economic policy have massively underestimated their true value, thereby paving the way for economic and ecological disaster in the near future, if they are taken seriously. By the essay's end, it will be clear that the costs of inviting orthodox economists into the climate-change debate greatly exceed the benefits of their contribution.

Chapter 4
The New Science of Societal Dynamics

The critical omission in the story about climate change is the science of societal dynamics. While there is a science of climate change – concerning the role played by human society in the recent increase in omissions and temperatures – there is no science of climate mitigation. The reason, as discussed in Chapter 3, is that orthodox economics has failed to develop a general dynamic theory of human society. Accordingly, the proposed mitigation program is based on wishful thinking rather than science. As such it is a metaphysical rather than a realist program. Hence, a new science of societal dynamics is urgently required.

THE NEW SCIENCE OUTLINED

This is not as daunting as it may at first appear. There already exists a realist general dynamic theory of human society, called the dynamic-strategy theory. Currently it is ignored by the mitigation engineers precisely because it is grounded in reality and, therefore, undermines their metaphysical vision. It is a transdisciplinary theory that has demonstrated its ability to explain and predict the core relationship in disciplines throughout the social, behavioral, biological and cognitive sciences.

What the dynamic-strategy theory shows is that life and human society are characterized by a series of biological and technological paradigm shifts, which are driven by the dynamic life-system. This life-system consists of a continuous process of circular interaction between its constituent organisms (including man) and the "society" of which they are a part. It is a self-starting and self-sustaining – or autogenous – system driven from the demand side by "strategic desire" – the desire of all organisms, no matter how simple or complex, to survive and prosper – and facilitated either by the "strategic gene" or the "strategic cerebrum", depending on their degree of sophistication. This theory has been developed over the past two decades.

The desire to survive and prosper leads to a pursuit of the most effective (at a particular time and place) dynamic strategy from an armory of four – family multiplication, conquest, commerce (symbiosis), or genetic/technological change. As the economic opportunities of these dynamic strategies are exploited by individual "strategists" (risk-taking decision makers) or groups of strategists, they unfold and generate a growing "strategic demand" for a wide range of inputs including factors of production (land, labor and capital), genetic or technological ideas, institutions (societal rules), organizations (social networks), religion, and culture. The supply response – shaped by relative factor prices – to strategic demand leads to the growing complexity of both biological/technological structures and the societal environment, and to an increase in biological/physical output and output per capita (or living standards).

This dynamic life-system emerged from primeval chaos in order to convert solar energy into fuels that facilitated the survival and ever-increasing complexity of life forms, including humanity. Over the past 4,000 myrs this life-system has developed into a highly robust and flexible "survival machine" able to exist in any extremely hostile environment. In the case of the human life-system, large and abrupt changes in climate over the past 100,000 years have conditioned it to withstand similar climate-change events in the future. It is a system that not only grows incrementally but also periodically transforms itself in a revolutionary way via what I call biological or technological paradigm shifts (see Figures 4.1 and 4.2). These paradigm shifts take the form of genetic or technological revolutions, which radically change the structure of the dynamic life-system and of its constituent ecosociopolitical systems. In the process they generate an exponential development path, which has been described by the Snooks-Panov algorithm (Nazaretyan 2005).

Figure 4.1 **The great steps of life – the past 4,000 myrs**

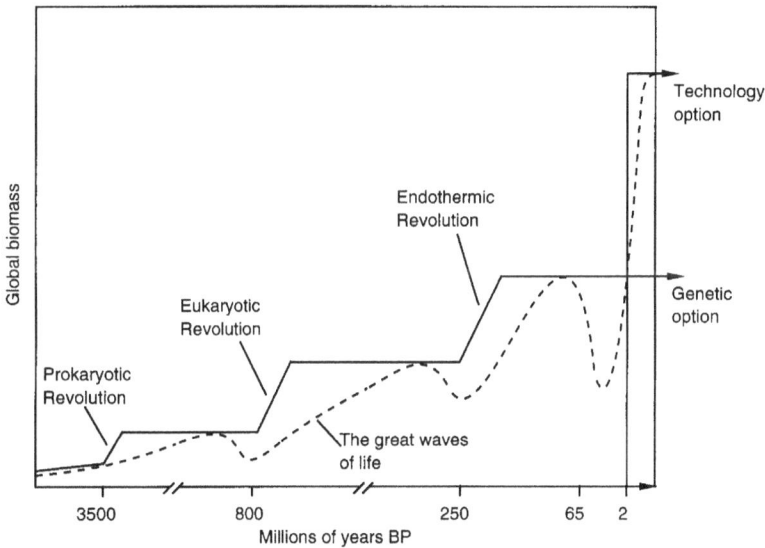

Source: Snooks 2003: 252

This realist theory, which is based on the systematic observation of natural and human life-systems, was first presented in my book *The Dynamic Society* (1996), and has been developed to apply to a wide variety of intellectual disciplines since then. More recently, the theory as it relates to the origin and evolution of life and its natural systems has been published in a number of scientific journals including *Advances in Space Research* (Snooks 2005) and *Complexity*

(Snooks 2008a). The focus in this chapter is on the dynamic-strategy theory as it applies to human society. A brief outline of the theory is followed by a discussion of the three technological paradigm shifts in the past, as well as the fourth paradigm shift that is predicted to begin in the middle decades of the twenty-first century.

A FORMAL PRESENTATION OF THE DYNAMIC-STRATEGY THEORY

To understand the patterns of societal dynamics in the long-run, we require a new dynamic theory. The old theories, unlike the dynamic patterns, tell a story of selective comparative statics. For this purpose the dynamic-strategy theory will be briefly outlined by focusing on its central features: the driving force; the dynamic mechanism; strategic demand and strategic confidence; the strategic demand-response mechanism; and strategic leadership in the Dynamic Society.

The driving force

The internal driving force of the Dynamic Society is the competitive struggle of "materialist man" to survive and prosper. This is the major outcome of our biologically determined desires – or "strategic desire" – that have been shaped by genetic change over almost 4,000 myrs. In the dynamic-strategy theory, as in life, ideas are an effective way of achieving our desires, but they do so in a passive way. In the long-run, as we will see, ideas respond to "strategic demand". Two major implications emerge from this reality: altruism is not a prime determinant of human behavior; and the decision-making process is not dominated by neoclassical economic rationality. The origin, evolution and nature of strategic demand and human nature have been explored in considerable depth in my recent book *The Selfcreating Mind* (2006a).

If ideas do not drive society, but merely facilitate the desire of its members, we need to replace the orthodox rationality model of decision making with a new realist model. Through the inductive method it is possible to derive such a model, which I have called the "strategic-imitation model" (Snooks 1996: 212–13; 1997: 36–46). In reality, decision making is based on the need to economize on nature's scarcest resource – intelligence. Rather than collect vast quantities of information on a large range of alternatives for processing through a mental model of the way the world works, the great majority of decision makers – whom I call the "strategic followers" – merely imitate those innovative people ("strategic pioneers") and projects that are conspicuously successful. The only information required is that necessary to answer the key questions: Who and what is materially successful and why? Hence, the basic information needed by decision makers is the relatively inexpensive "imitative information", not the prohibitively expensive benefit-cost information. Even the leading decision makers – the strategic pioneers – do not employ rationalist techniques when seeking new ways of exploiting strategic opportunities. Rather than exhaustively seeking out the best investment projects, they *believe* their investment projects are best. In free-enterprise societies – but not the "mitigation society" – it is the market that adjudicates.

The dynamic mechanism

The internal driving force of strategic demand is a self-starting and self-sustaining force that drives a dynamic mechanism that has at its centre the "strategic pursuit" – the pursuit of a dominant dynamic strategy to achieve the objective of survival and prosperity. This strategy begins as an individual or family activity that, if successful, is adopted by wider social groups, at first local, then regional, national and, finally, global. This takes place through the mechanism of "strategic imitation", whereby successful pioneering initiatives are imitated by a growing number of individuals and groups. In this way, a successful dynamic strategy becomes the focus of political policies controlled by ruling strategists, or "strategic leaders". The role of "strategic leadership", which is not to be confused with "mitigation engineering", is discussed below.

The choice of dynamic strategy – from four possibilities including family multiplication (procreation *and* migration), conquest, commerce, and technological change – depends on the underlying economic conditions, such as factor endowments and the nature of external competition. A few examples will clarify what this meant in practice. Family-expansion societies include *all* societies prior to the Neolithic (agricultural) Revolution 10,600 years ago; commerce societies include Egypt, Phoenicia, Greece, Carthage, Byzantium, Venice, pre-modern Britain, and the Netherlands; conquest societies include most of the ancient world, such as Sumer, Assyria, Babylon, Persia, Rome, the Arab empires, the Mongol empires, medieval Europe, and Mesoamerican societies; and technological societies include all those that since the late eighteenth century have passed through the Industrial Revolution.

It is a choice about the future made by strategists who invest time and resources in alternative dynamic strategies. The important point to realize is that investment in these various strategies is undertaken for the same objective – survival and prosperity – and involves a broadly similar process, which is the strategic pursuit. The main difference is that investment in family multiplication, conquest and commerce is undertaken in order to achieve economic growth by gaining control of new *external* resources, while technological change is used to achieve economic growth by effecting greater efficiency in the use of existing *internal* resources. As far as the strategist is concerned – in contrast to the orthodox economist – there is nothing special about technological change. After all, economic growth in Roman society for a period of 1,000 years was generated knowingly through the systematic pursuit of conquest, not technological change. Technological change, like the other three dynamic strategies, is just an instrument in the more general strategic pursuit. Similarly, within the context of a particular dynamic strategy, strategists attempt to gain a competitive advantage through the adoption of new substrategies that, where successful, generate new "technological styles", such as the simple mechanical technology adopted by Britain between 1780 and 1830 or the more sophisticated chemical and electrical technology employed by Germany during the mid-nineteenth century.

As individuals and governments seek to exploit their physical and societal environment, setting in train a mass movement orchestrated through strategic imitation, the dominant dynamic strategy unfolds. Unfolds in the sense that its material opportunities are progressively exploited and, finally, exhausted. And it is this unfolding dynamic strategy (or a substrategy of it) that shapes the expectations of decision makers. The eventual exhaustion of a dynamic strategy is the outcome of the "law of diminishing *strategic* returns", whereby the revenue and costs of *strategies* rather than factors of production are finally equated (Snooks 1998a: 202–03). The resulting "rise and fall" of dynamic strategies and substrategies traces out a distinctive wave-like pathway (see Figure 4.4), which provides the dynamic form for this model. This supersedes the arbitrary dynamic forms – the equilibrium growth path and the bifurcated pathways – adopted by supply-side neoclassical, evolutionary, and complexity growth theorists. A meaningful dynamic form cannot be deduced logically from supply-side assumptions about society. It is an existential concept, not an optimizing concept.

From historical observations, however, we can derive a general dynamic form that encompasses a series of wave-like surges in economic development and growth that are separated by intervals of stability or retreat. This sequence consists of "great waves" of about 300 years in duration and, within these, "long waves" of about 30–60 years. The great waves are generated by the exploitation and exhaustion of dynamic strategies (for example, the present industrial technology strategy) and the long waves by a series of substrategies (for example, the pioneering phase of the Industrial Revolution in Britain, 1780–1830). We should focus, however, on the underlying dynamic mechanism rather than the precise wave-like pattern, because external shocks (such as invasion, disease, and physical calamities) continually distort the latter. These wave-like surges should not be thought of as part of a dynamic "cycle", because the intervals between them are not systematically related to the surges of development before and after. Each of these intervals constitutes a hiatus that follows the exhaustion of a dynamic strategy (or substrategy) during which the strategists search desperately for a replacement strategy (or substrategy). The best recent example of such a strategic hiatus is Japan during the 1990s and early 2000s; and a possible future case could be the USA. If the strategists are successful the strategic sequence will continue with a replacement strategy, but, if not, the sequence will terminate and the society will eventually collapse. The latter ultimately occurred in all ancient societies.

Strategic demand and strategic confidence

The unfolding dynamic strategy, driven by the competitive energy of strategic demand ("materialist man"), plays a central role in the dynamic-strategy model. Not only does it provide the model with a realistic dynamic form, but it gives rise to two new concepts in economics – "strategic confidence" and "strategic demand". These concepts explain not only the dynamics of long-run investment and saving that are left hanging in orthodox comparative-static macroeconomics, but also how "dynamic order" (usually called spontaneous order) is generated. It is the exploration of the demand side of dynamics that makes the dynamic-strategy theory unique in a world of supply-side theories, not only in economics and the other social sciences, but also in biology and physics (Snooks 2008a).

What do I mean by demand-side and supply-side theories? Supply-side theories model societal outcomes as if they are forced by the prime resources (largely human) of a country, whereas the dynamic-strategy theory models these outcomes as a response of society's resources to the driving influence of dynamic demand generated by an unfolding dynamic strategy. For example, the pursuit of the commerce strategy by, say, Venice in the pre-modern period, generated a continuously changing demand for a wide variety of inputs – commercial capital, commercial expertise, shipping, docks and warehousing, overseas ports peopled by skilled Venetians, commercial inventions, and a variety of commercial institutions and organizations – to fully exploit its monopoly over trade between Western Europe on the one hand and Byzantium and the Levant on the other. Supply side-ists would argue that Venice grew rich because of its superior commercial human capital, owing to something special about its culture (such as its religion or Roman inheritance).

Strategic confidence, which rises and falls with the dominant dynamic strategy and its various substrategies, explains the changing investment climate in the Dynamic Society. It provides, for example, a dynamic explanation for Keynes' "state of long-term expectation". Accordingly it plays a central role in determining the willingness of strategists to invest, because of its influence on the long-run expected rate of return, and in the creation of dynamic order (through encouraging cooperation and an orderly institutional structure). Confidence and expectations rise as the dynamic strategy unfolds, and they decline, stagnate, and may even collapse as it is progressively exhausted. It is important to realize that strategic confidence is unaffected by the speculative excesses of the stock exchange (the "casino") or of the financial sector, as these are merely ephemeral supply-side disturbances (Snooks 2008d). Strategic confidence also binds society together.

Strategic demand – or dynamic demand – also waxes and wanes with the dominant dynamic strategy or substrategy. It comprises the effective demand exercised by decision makers for a wide range of physical, intellectual and institutional inputs required in the strategic pursuit. In exploiting expanding strategic opportunities, entrepreneurs need to invest in new infrastructure; to purchase intermediate goods and services; to employ labor skills; to acquire, renovate, or construct the necessary buildings, machinery, and equipment; to engage professional expertise; and to develop new facilitating social rules and organizations. *Strategic demand, therefore, is the central active principle in our demand-side model.* Naturally the supply response of population change, capital formation, technological change, and institutional transformation, which are influenced by changes in relative prices, will contribute to the way in which strategic opportunities are exploited; but they do so passively. This concept turns Say's Law – which was accepted explicitly by the classical economists and implicitly by neoclassical economists – on its head: in the Dynamic Society, dynamic demand creates its own supply, not the other way around.

The strategic demand-supply response

With the dynamic-strategy model we can shift focus from short-run, comparative-static macroeconomics to long-run dynamics by considering the interaction between strategic demand and the response of the supply-side variables. It is this interaction that causes the dynamic strategy to unfold and, hence, gives rise to the dynamic form of our model, and to the dynamic role played by *strategic* inflation in facilitating the supply response. "Strategic inflation" – or "good" inflation – is the widespread increase in prices resulting from the pressure of strategic demand on resources, commodities, and ideas. With the introduction of a new dynamic strategy/substrategy, the resulting expansion of strategic demand will lead to an increase in prices of key inputs, but will not generate strategic inflation until the new strategy exerts widespread influence throughout a given society. Economic growth of a traditional and unadventurous (that is, nonstrategic) kind that occurs within the context of known and available resources may not lead to much inflation at all. But this nonstrategic growth will not last for long. "Nonstrategic inflation" – or "bad" inflation – on the other hand, is the increase of prices resulting from errors in monetary and fiscal policy or the action of monopolies in either factor or commodity markets at home and abroad.

Herein lie the major differences between strategic theory and orthodox theory. In neoclassical economics the supply side is, by default, treated as the active force in society (supply creates it own demand), which has no place for strategic inflation; while in Keynesian economics the supply-side variables are merely assumed to be given and "effective demand" is a comparative-static, national-accounting concept. By contrast, in the dynamic-strategy model, strategic demand provides the active force to which the supply-side variables respond according to their supply costs. Strategic inflation, which provides the incentive system in this strategic demand-response mechanism, is a stable, non-accelerating function of economic growth. This theoretical relationship can be (and has been) estimated in the form of the "growth-inflation curve" over all timeframes – including the very long-run (past 1,000 years), the long-run (past 100 years), and shortrun (1960s–1990s). These growth-inflation curves are estimated and discussed in my book *Longrun Dynamics* (1998b: 151–59). Inflation targeting, where this constrains strategic inflation (as it invariably does), acts as a brake on the unfolding dynamic strategy, as occurred dramatically around the globe in 2008–09. To eliminate strategic inflation in the long-run is to eliminate economic growth. Hence, it is fascinating that in the *Stern Report*, stabilization targeting is a concept based on the bankrupt idea of inflation targeting, because both work to undermine the dynamic mechanism driving human society.

Population, labor supply, capital formation, and technological, institutional and cultural ideas all respond to the unfolding dynamic strategy. Changes in these supply-side variables, both in terms of composition and growth rates, are a function of changing strategic opportunities. These variables expand and become more complex as the dominant dynamic strategy is exploited; and they stagnate, decline, and lose purpose, as the dynamic strategy is progressively exhausted and marginal *strategic* returns decline. Rapidly rising and falling prices form the catalyst for these dynamic developments. Naturally, supply-side costs play a role in shaping the strategic response, but this is a passive rather than an active role. Difficulties of supply are met by substitution of other resources and/or by innovation. In this way the supply-side variables are internalized in the dynamic-strategy model. Dynamic demand creates its own supply, and, in the process, creates the technological development pathway. Large-scale interventions, as proposed by the IPCC, Stern, and others, will merely subvert this dynamic process.

The role of strategic leadership

Strategic leadership, which is also a response to strategic demand, is essential to the survival and prosperity of human society. It was the primary reason for the emergence of government at the dawn of civilization and for its extension and maintenance ever since. Basically it involves *facilitating* the objectives of society's dynamic strategists by coordinating their efforts and *not by setting these objectives or compelling the strategists to comply* as required by the mitigation engineers. In particular the strategic state provides basic infrastructure required by the unfolding dynamic strategy that is beyond the risk threshold and financial resources of individual and corporations; it negotiates political and commercial deals with other societies; it protects the dynamic strategy at home and abroad; it encourages the emergence of new strategies during recessions/depressions; and it provides basic facilities for education, training and research required to nourish the long-term health of the prevailing dynamic strategy, whether it be conquest, commerce, or technological change. This is a proactive rather than a passive role, and *it is undertaken by the representatives of the strategists for the benefit of the strategists.* This is discussed in detail in my books *The Ephemeral Civilization* (1997: 54–8) and *The Global Crisis Makers* (2000: 59–111).

It is important to realize that the strategists do not necessarily encompass the entire population of a society. They include only those individuals who invest in the dominant dynamic strategy, either in physical or human-capital terms. The proportion of the population that can be classified as being among the strategists has varied throughout human history, not in a linear but in a circular way (Snooks 1997: ch. 3). In paleolithic (hunter-gatherer) society, almost 100 percent of adult members were actively involved in the family-multiplication strategy (for example, Aboriginal Australia). Hence, family and tribal leaders had to take into consideration the aspirations of all adults. By contrast, in neolithic (agricultural) societies, only a small proportion of the population was actively engaged in the strategic pursuit, while the great majority were nonstrategists, being deprived of their liberty by the ruling elite. The proportion of strategists in the population ranged from less than 1 percent in conquest societies (for example, Anglo-Norman England) to about one-quarter in commerce societies (ancient Greece or medieval Venice). Only in advanced technological societies has the strategist/population ratio once more approached that of hunter-gatherer societies. Curiously the close historical relationship between dynamic strategists and their leaders has, since the 1970s, broken down in the modern world. And with this breakdown of strategic leadership, governments have neglected modern technological dynamic strategies in favor of military adventurism in the Middle East, Georgia, and elsewhere. They have also been seduced by interventionist notions of an antistrategic kind, such as climate mitigation and large-scale financial support of failing corporations.

Metaphysics poses a great threat to the age-old positive role of strategic leadership. Under the influence of the neoliberals and neo-conservatives, the facilitating role of strategic leadership has been belittled and perverted to support military adventures in various parts of the world. On the other hand, under the influence of the mitigation engineers, there has arisen a new demand for a change in the role of government leadership. The introduction and maintenance of their climate-mitigation program requires governments to *hijack rather than facilitate* the strategic pursuit by taking the age-old initiative away from the strategists in order to set society's goals, directions, incentives and technologies – under the guidance of the mitigationists of course. They want governments to substitute metaphysical goals for strategic goals and to assume responsibility for driving the introduction and development of low-carbon technologies. As shown in Chapter 5, this is a recipe for disaster. Now we turn to the exponential technological pathway.

THE EXPONENTIAL TECHNOLOGICAL PATHWAY

By employing both the observed patterns of history and the general dynamic-strategy model we can identify and explain the three great interlocking mechanisms of the Dynamic Society that have been operating over the past two million years. Our general model generates distinct but related processes of economic change in different historical circumstances. But even these different circumstances are related to each other by an overarching global dynamic structure. This is the "technological pathway" consisting of "great technological paradigm shifts" (see Figure 4.2) that have been occurring at geometrically diminishing intervals since the emergence of mankind in the form of the paleolithic (hunting), neolithic (agricultural), and industrial (modern) revolutions. Within this global dynamic structure, the dominant mechanisms of change are the "great dispersion" during the paleolithic era, the "great wheel of civilization" during the neolithic era, and the "great linear waves of economic change" during the modern era. Each of these mechanisms of transformation, driven by the materialist pursuit of dynamic strategies, has carried human society towards the upper limits of the prevailing technological paradigm and, hence, to a new technological paradigm shift. This exponential technological development path was generated despite the onset of a significant number of large and abrupt climate-change episodes, owing to the growing resilience of the dynamic life-system.

Figure 4.2 **The great steps of human progress – the past 2 myrs**

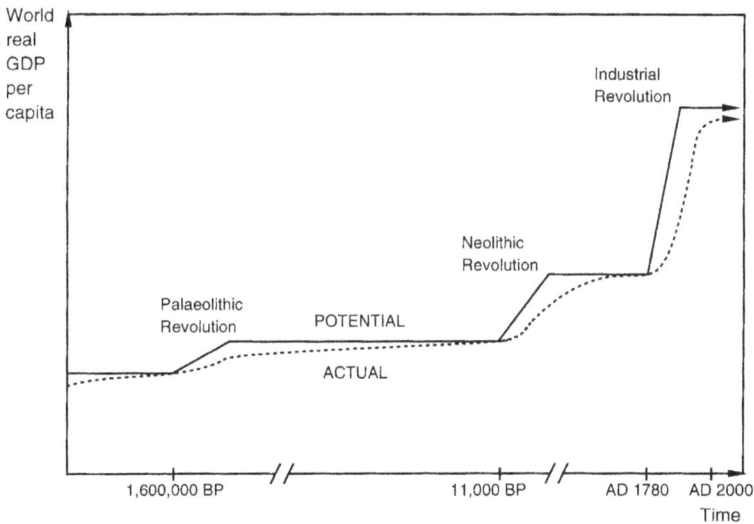

Source: Snooks 1996: 403

A global dynamic structure

As shown in *The Dynamic Society* (1996: ch. 12), the process by which global technological paradigm shifts emerge is accelerating in a geometric fashion. The time taken for the technological shifts to occur involved hundreds of thousands of years for the Paleolithic, 4,000 years for the Neolithic, and 100 years for the Industrial Revolution. The time taken to transmit these new paradigms around the known world was about 1.2 million years for the Paleolithic, 3,000 plus years for the Old-World Neolithic, and 200 plus years for the Industrial Revolution. And the interval between the Paleolithic and Neolithic revolutions was about 2 million years, whereas that between the Neolithic and Industrial Revolutions was about 10,000 years. The reason for this global acceleration is that the outputs of one round of technological change become the inputs of the next.

The global development path implied by the great technological paradigm shifts can be illustrated by reference to Figure 4.2, which encompasses all societies in the known world in the history of human society. It is designed to show two things: the stepped profile of *potential* real GDP per capita at the global level made possible by the three paradigm shifts (heavy line); and the more gradual increase in *actual* real GDP per capita (broken line). Potential GDP per capita increases relatively steeply – becoming more steep as we approach the present – but is then stationary for much longer periods that diminish geometrically over time. By contrast, actual GDP per capita increases only gradually to the potential ceiling and describes a more wave-like development path. This catching-up process by actual GDP per capita is driven by the three great mechanisms discussed more fully below. Once global resources have been fully employed in the current technological paradigm, actual income will press persistently against the potential ceiling. This is when the next technological revolution takes place, because the alternative is stagnation and collapse for the leading global societies. Humanity will face precisely this transforming situation in the middle decades of the twenty-first century.

The great dispersion

The first historical mechanism to drive a technological paradigm shift was the great dispersion of the paleolithic era. This involved the adoption of the extremely slow but very effective dynamic strategy of family multiplication (of procreation *and* migration) to enable greater family control over unused natural resources, which were utilized through a hunter-gathered technology. This great dispersion probably began in Africa about 100,000 years ago. By 40,000 years ago modern man had reached most parts of the globe, and by 11,000 years ago in the Old World and 7,000 years ago in the New World all resources had been fully utilized – the paleolithic ceiling of potential GDP per capita had been reached. This pressure on resources was most intense in those narrow necks of land – which I call "funnels of transformation" – through which relatively large numbers of people passed, where population density was relatively high, and where competition was more intense. In the fertile crescent of the Old World and the Mesoamerican isthmus of the New World the incentives for adopting new ways of using scarce resources were greatest. These were the cradles of the Neolithic Revolution.

The great wheel of civilization

The mechanism driving the technological paradigm shift between the Neolithic and Modern eras was what I call the "great wheel of civilization". Each rotation of the great wheel brought the Dynamic Society closer to the limit of the old neolithic paradigm through population expansion and the transmission of ideas. This dynamic process, which underlies the rise and fall of ancient civilizations in both the Old and New Worlds, was in turn driven by the dynamic strategy of conquest. The reason for the eternal recurrence of the ancient world is that the conqueror must rebuild his empire anew on each and every occasion. Only through the modern technological strategy can the great wheel be broken and civilization be set free to pursue a sustained linear development path. Yet even this escape will not be permanent if we forget how we broke away and allow the mitigation engineers to lock us into the old polluting fossil-fuel paradigm.

The great wheel of ancient civilization rotates slowly in historical space without gaining the technological traction required to drive global GDP per capita upwards over the long-run. In Figure 4.3, four great wheels of economic growth have been arbitrarily depicted, each of which represents a single ancient Western civilization in a series of successions – Sumer, Assyria, Greece, and Rome. While the diameters of the wheels are slightly different owing to a marginal improvement in living standards over time as military and organizational structures became more efficient, they have a common axis, which is fixed by a shared production technology. It is well known that, while military technology changed significantly over these three millennia, production technology changed only marginally.

Figure 4.3 **The great wheel of civilization**

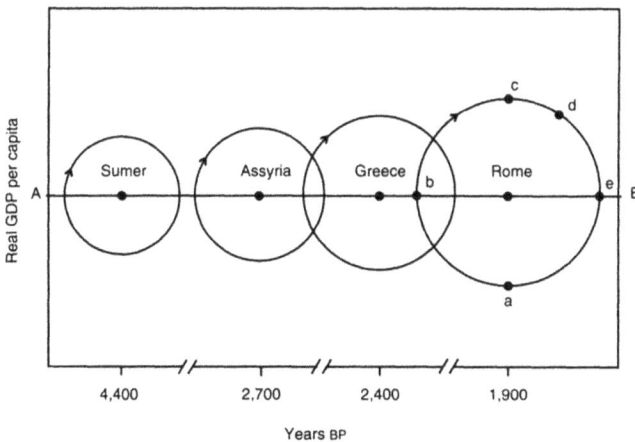

Source: Snooks 1996: 407

How does the "great-wheel" diagram work? It is important to realize that while the "great-steps" diagram (Figure 4.2) operates at the global level, the "great-wheel" diagram (Figure 4.3) operates at the level of the individual society; and that time on the horizontal axis is not continuous (that is, time cannot move back on itself). Each rotation of the great wheel for these societies took between one and two millennia. We start at the low point of the wheel. The origin, *a*, of each civilization is small and unimpressive and, with the exception of the pioneering society of Sumer, is overshadowed by its predecessor. As the internal energy of materialist man is translated into economic expansion through, initially, family multiplication, the incipient core of our new civilization borrows ideas and techniques from its predecessor and applies these to its expansion process. As real GDP per capita grows, the great wheel begins to turn slowly anew. Once our society has borrowed all it can from the past, the wheel has reached point *b*, the maximum level of real GPD per capita that can be generated from the neolithic economic system common to the ancient world.

This is a critical point at which the great wheel could stop, and even rotate backwards. The most cost-effective way of maintaining positive economic growth in ancient societies – of maintaining the upward swing of the great wheel – is through the adoption of the dynamic strategy of conquest. Only a fortunate few were able to achieve this through commerce (the Archaic Greeks and the Phoenicians) and even these were eventually overwhelmed by conquest societies. For a successful conquest strategy, the great wheel continues to rotate upwards from *b* to *c* as the flow of plundered income and resources from outside increases. But, inevitably, the conquest (or commerce) strategy is exhausted (when *strategic* benefits and costs are equated), the inflow of external resources dries up, and the former conquest society is thrown back on its own internal resources. Hence, the great wheel begins to rotate downwards to *d* and beyond. The stationary state is not possible in a highly competitive world. As the underlying neolithic production technology is not sufficient to support such high living standards and populations, the great wheel rotates from *d* to *e*, and eventually disintegrates (back to *a*) as Rome did between AD 200 and 476, and as the modern world will do if the mitigation engineers have their way.

The great linear waves of economic change

The Industrial Revolution not only ushered in a new technological paradigm, it also began a new era in which linear, if fluctuating, economic growth was possible (see Figure 4.4). This was unprecedented in human history. The great linear waves of economic change are generated by the modern technological strategy (or component substrategies), and they are responsible for driving the modern industrial technological paradigm to exhaustion and, if the mitigation engineers can be restrained, to a new technological dawn.

Figure 4.4 **The great waves of change, England 1000–2000**

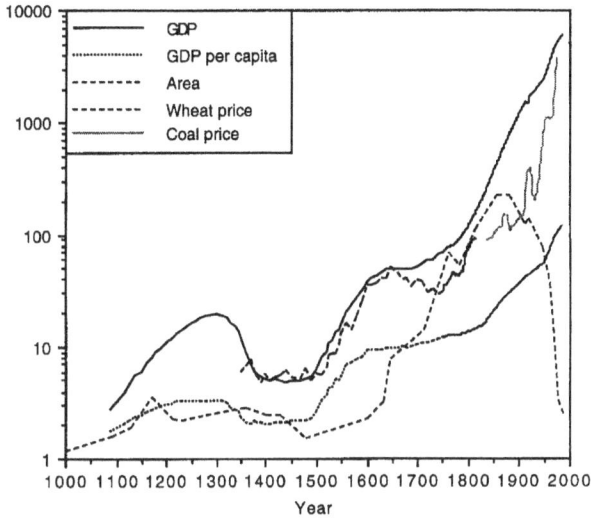

Source: Snooks 1997: 276

It is important to realize that these wave-like surges of about 300 years are not systematically related in some sort of mechanical way as orthodox trade-cycle theory might, if it recognized them, claim. In reality there is no system of very long cycles. The intervals between these great waves are just that – intervals between the exhaustion of one dynamic strategy and the emergence and exploitation of another. During each of these intervals – a period of "hiatus" – the strategic pioneers are involved in a desperate attempt to launch a new strategy owing to the adverse impact of external competition on real living standards. Each hiatus is a vulnerable time for any society, because strategic replacement is not inevitable. Failure to generate a new strategy will lead a society to stagnate and, possibly, collapse. It is for this reason I stress that modern linear development takes place through a succession of *unsystematic* "waves" rather than through mechanical cycles in which downturn and contraction are followed necessarily by upturn and expansion.

The precise length of these waves, measured not from peak to peak as in trade cycles but from trough to peak as in wave-like fluctuations, should not concern us greatly. My research for *The Dynamic Society* (1996) and *The Ephemeral Civilization* (1997) suggests that the upswing of the "great waves" (reflecting the unfolding of full dynamic strategies) in both the ancient and modern worlds is *about* 300 years in duration, and of the "long waves" (reflecting the unfolding of substrategies) is *about* 30 to 60 years. Random external shocks help to distort this pattern. Far more important is the dynamic mechanism that underlies these wave-like surges. Any predictions we are prepared to make about economic progress in the future must be based on the underlying dynamic model, and the laws that can be derived from it, rather than on fixed (and, hence, inevitably wrong) assertions about wave length. Much of the recent (and distant) literature has focused, mistakenly, on the predictive value of cycle length. As a result it has been largely discredited (Solomou 1987). This is the old historicist fallacy revisited – not for the only time in our survey of the conventional wisdom, as we saw in chapters 2 and 3.

THE STRATEGIC MODEL OF INSTITUTIONAL CHANGE

Societal rules (or "institutions"), both formal (laws) and informal (customs), are established and altered to facilitate the dynamic strategies by which decision makers attempt to maximize their chances of survival and prosperity, and to impose the dynamic tactics by which competing groups attempt to control the distribution of society's wealth. These rules are required to economize not on cost-benefit information as Douglass North (1990) and the new institutionalists assert but on nature's scarcest resource – the intellect. Similarly, societal "organizations" of all types – economic, political, and social – also largely respond to these dynamic strategies and tactics, rather than to institutions as the new institutionalists suggest. Society's institutions and organizations, therefore, are driven not by some sort of evolutionary process, as commonly claimed, but by strategic demand that arises from the unfolding of the dominant dynamic strategy. Social evolution is a myth.

Strategic demand provides the incentives, opportunities and imperatives for the changing – the ephemeral – structure of civilization. As shown in *The Ephemeral Civilization* (1997), the strategic phases of adoption, expansion, decline and exhaustion have a characteristic impact on observed changes in the institutional/organizational structure of society. Institutional change has no life of its own. It cannot evolve in isolation from what is happening in the real economy. It is reactive not proactive, facilitating not initiating. It has no evolutionary logic and, therefore, no laws of its own. This is why we need not take the excited ephemeral gyrations of the financial sector (as in the second half of 2008) too seriously (Snooks 2008d).

If the long-run "strategic sequence" were to reverse itself, the sociopolitical structure would also do so. The only reason that the last millennium in Britain gives the impression that democratic sociopolitical institutions and organizations have "evolved" is that the strategic sequence has been conquest → commerce → technological change (the reason for this is discussed in *The Ephemeral Civilization*, 1997: 338–340). Had it been conquest → commerce → conquest as it was throughout the premodern period (for example, ancient Greece and medieval Venice), then the growing democratization of the middle, commerce phase would have been turned back to autocracy once more. The same will happen in the future if our current technological strategy is replaced by a conquest strategy (as occurred in Germany and Japan in the mid twentieth century), by, for example, a fanatical climate-change dictator. This, of course, is not possible in the evolutionary model, where non-marginal change is irreversible. In the end it must be recognized that human civilization is merely a vehicle for achieving the basic desires of mankind, and that, while the dynamic process is eternal, the rites of civilization are ephemeral.

The central mechanism of institutional change in the dynamic-strategy model is the competitive struggle between various groups in society for control of the dominant dynamic strategy. This is the struggle between strategists, nonstrategists and antistrategists: of which the most recent example is that between the antistrategic (metaphysical) mitigation engineers and the strategic (realist) corporate sector. The only reason modern societies possess democratic sociopolitical institutions is that their entire populations have been drawn into the ruling strategic group. This has not been a linear, but a circular, historical development. As suggested earlier, whereas in hunger-gatherer societies most of their populations were strategists, in conquest societies the landowning warriors constituted a tiny ruling elite, in commerce societies their ruling class was extended to include the mercantile middle class, and in technological societies the ruling class embraced, once more, the bulk of the population who invested funds and/or skills in the modern dynamic strategy. The way this works is discussed in detail in *The Ephemeral Civilization* (1997).

The point I am trying to make is that, as there is no independent dynamic mechanism underlying institutional change, there can be no independent laws governing it. The great quest of the new institutionalists to discover a general model of societal rules, therefore, is futile. It is a quest for the Holy Grail. While there certainly are regularities, or recurring patterns, in institutional formation throughout space and time – such as between the conquest societies of Assyria or Rome or the commerce societies of Greece and Carthage – they are the outcome of the real economy's dynamic and not of any independent institutional mechanism. Hence, the laws of institutional change must be derived from the fundamental laws of social dynamics. The ephemeral nature of civilization can only be understood in terms of the eternal forces that drive the Dynamic Society.

A NEW SCIENCE OF SOCIETY

As shown in Chapter 3, orthodox economics, usually considered to be "at the cutting edge of the social sciences" (Wilson 1999: 219), has nothing of significance to say about the past and future dynamics of human society. Hence, the only way to understand the future role of climate change, generally acknowledged to reflect modern human activities, is by developing a new science of society – what I call the science of stratology. The foundation for this new science is the dynamic-strategy theory outlined above.

In this chapter I have attempted to show that the dynamic-strategy theory has enabled the identification of the dynamic life-system that makes it possible for life forms to survive and prosper in a hostile world – including a world subject to abrupt and rapid climate change. As this system is self-starting and self-sustaining, it doesn't require any external interventions to ensure it operates properly. The dynamic life-system establishes its own goals, directions and incentives and communicates these via strategic demand for a range of strategic inputs through various markets and attendant price mechanisms. The failure to understand the presence and operation of the dynamic life-system has led metaphysicians of various types – including Marxists and mitigation engineers – to propose artificial goals and the directives and incentives for achieving them. This has the very real potential for distorting, even derailing, the dynamic life-system, with disastrous consequences.

The societal theory outlined in this chapter provides a way of thinking about the dynamic life-system and how it generates the development patterns of the past and future. In particular, how it generates the technological development path that proceeds via a series of geometrically related paradigm shifts. It is the knowledge this theory provides that is essential to an understanding of the pattern of societal dynamics and its interaction with climate change. It provides the basis for a new science of societal dynamics. In Chapter 5, this knowledge enables us to calculate a *realist* version of likely greenhouse-gas concentrations, of human-induced temperature changes, of the benefits of "allowing" the dynamic life-system to work unhindered so as to generate the fourth technological paradigm shift – the Solar Revolution – and of the real costs of the proposed comprehensive climate-mitigation program.

Chapter 5
Mitigation or Revolution? The Real Costs and Benefits

In this chapter two alternative futures for humanity are outlined. The first involves the future that would be generated by the dynamic life-system free to do what it does best – ensure the survival and prosperity of life forms in a hostile physical world. The second is that proposed by the mitigation engineers, who are completely unaware of the presence or operation of the dynamic life-system either in the past or in the future: namely the introduction of a comprehensive climate-mitigation program that will distort, even derail, the dynamic life-system, and inevitably delay, even completely prevent, the emergence of the fourth technological paradigm shift. In effect this will involve a future clash between the antistrategic mitigation engineers and the global strategists, similar in nature but potentially much more destructive than the clash between the antistrategists (USSR and China) and the strategists (the Western powers) during the Cold War. Whatever decision humanity makes in this respect, we should be aware of the likely consequences of our actions.

THE SOLAR REVOLUTION

When the dynamic-strategy theory was first published in *The Dynamic Society* (1996) – but actually worked out in the early 1990s – I made a number of predictions about the future technological development path for human society that are relevant to the climate-change debate. At the time there was a concern among the radical ecologists – who I called the "ecological engineers" – that population growth, which they wrongly viewed as an increasing function of economic growth, was irreparably damaging the natural environment and, thereby, leading to the inevitable collapse of human society. These doomsters included the "limits-to-growth" people (Meadows et al 1972; 1992) together with radical ecologists such as Paul Ehrlich (*The Population Explosion*, 1990) and David Suzuki (1990). They demanded that human society "immediately" attempt to live within its physical limits by eliminating economic growth, which, they incorrectly claimed, was driving population growth, which was destroying the planet. If we failed to do this "immediately" human society would collapse sometime during the early part of the twenty-first century. These predictions were based, at best, on simple engineering models (with feedback effects) that extrapolate certain key variables into the future on the assumptions that appeared relevant to the ecological engineers at the time (Snooks 1996: 103–110). As the dynamic-strategy theory shows, population growth is a response, via strategic demand, to the type of dynamic strategy being pursued, not to economic growth. While earlier dynamic strategies of family multiplication, commerce, and conquest required population growth to feed the unfolding strategic process, the current dynamic strategy of technological change does not because it is able to extract increasing services from a given supply of labor and resources. At heart, these historicist models have much in common with those used by climate-change scientists and orthodox economists today.

The Dynamic Society (Snooks 1996) identified problems with both these models and the assumed relationship between variables like economic growth and population change. In particular, it was demonstrated that these models were not based on a realist general dynamic model and, as a consequence, could not foresee the forthcoming technological revolution that would enable human society to break through the alleged physical "limits to growth". As it turned out, global economic growth did not abate – in fact it increased owing to the rapid development achieved by China, India, and Southeast Asia, at a time of continued growth in the West. Despite this, the world was not overwhelmed with population, and the dynamics of human society did not crash as the ecological engineers predicted. After the turn of the century, it became more widely recognized that there was no simple relationship between the growth of both living standards and population, just as had been shown theoretically and empirically in my books *The Dynamic Society* (1996), *The Ephemeral Civilization* (1997), and *Global Transition* (1999).

Owing to the failure of their predictions of disaster, and the irrelevance of their theoretical models, the limits-to-growth groups (including the radical ecologists like Ehrlich and Suzuki) just withered away. Only to be replaced by the climate-change fraternity, using more sophisticated versions of the same historicist models that are also unable to capture the dynamics of human society or predict the forthcoming technological paradigm shift. When pushed, the climate-change people also display the old anti-growth and anti-population sentiments, but, owing to the failure of their predecessors, they express these flawed ideas more carefully.

Here is what I said about the forthcoming technological revolution in *The Dynamic Society* (1996: 429):

> In Chapter 9 it was shown that the distance between paradigm shifts and their duration has been declining in a geometric fashion. The time taken for the technological shifts to occur involved hundreds of thousands of years for the Paleolithic (c. 1.6 myrs ago), 4,000 years for the Neolithic (10,600 years ago), and 100 years for the Industrial (c. 1760) Revolutions. This suggests that the next paradigm shift could begin soon and could be completed in no more than a generation or so. The future revolution, as history has suggested, will release population from the present resources limit and, as a result, actually *reduce* environmental degradation. This is because it will no longer be necessary to push natural resources to their limits with an increasingly restricted technology, and because higher levels of real GDP per capita in the Third World will lead to a levelling-off of population, as has already occurred in developed nations ... The

present concerns about overpopulation and environment degradation, therefore, will be overcome by the future technological paradigm shift ... But this is not to say that we should abandon attempts to protect the environment, just that we should not allow this remedial action to derail the Dynamic Society.

In the early 1990s, armed with the dynamic-strategy theory, it was clear to me that the industrial technological paradigm had already entered its exhaustion phase, and would be replaced in the middle decades of the twenty-first century by a new technological paradigm. The degradation of the environment that was of concern to the ecologists at the time was a sign of this. Their error was to read the evidence of paradigm exhaustion as signs of ecological and societal collapse, and this error was an outcome of the failure to develop a general dynamic theory of human society. As I said in *The Dynamic Society* (Snooks 1996: 428–29), the radical ecologists

> by persuading even a significant proportion of individuals and global organisations that the historically familiar signs of a technological paradigm approaching exhaustion are instead the signs of a world teetering on the edge of darkness ... may do considerable and unnecessary damage. Through costly and unnecessary government intervention at the national and global levels, they may contribute both to the weakening of Western civilization ... and to the delay in any future technological paradigm shift.

Since the early 1990s, other evidence of an exhausting technological paradigm has emerged. This includes the rapidly diminishing supplies of fossil fuels – particularly petroleum – available at economic prices, and the growing costs of reducing the carbon emitted by their use in production, heating, and transport. In response to the potential energy-supply problems, industrialized countries are already positioning themselves strategically to secure oil supplies. These countries include the USA in the Middle East and Russia in Georgia. These wars are all about diminishing supplies of oil, not about "terrorism", "weapons of mass destruction", the existence of brutal dictators, or the rights of nationals in neighboring countries.

It is worth considering the situation regarding global oil and coal supplies in greater detail owing to the central role they play in providing energy in the industrial technological paradigm. The signs that the "golden age of oil" has passed have been accumulating for some time. In 1962 the global discovery of *new* oil fields peaked; in 1970 total oil production peaked in the USA (something the industry in the 1950s said could not happen), Venezuela and Libya; in the 1970s, 1980s and 1990s it peaked in Iran, Canada (conventional supplies), Romania, Indonesia, Egypt, India, Syria, Gabon, Malaysia, Argentina, Colombia, Ecuador and Great Britain; and in the early years of the twenty-first century these countries were joined by Norway, Oman, Mexico and Australia. Of the remaining oil producers, Kuwait is expected to peak in 2013, Saudi Arabia in 2014, and Iraq in 2018. While China and Canada (exploiting oil sands) are expanding production rapidly, they too are expected to peak before

2020. Although the data are difficult to assess accurately, many observers (see *Energy Bulletin*) believe that global oil production has either peaked or is about to peak.

With the passing of global peak oil production and the exponential growth of world demand – driven particularly by the rapid industrialization of China, India, and Southeast Asia – cheap oil will quickly become a thing of the past. Certainly by the middle decades of the twenty-first century, oil reserves will be unable to support civilization as we know it (Hirsch 2005), *if we become trapped in the current industrial technological paradigm.*

What of coal, that other energy mainstay of the industrial paradigm? The situation with coal is less clear owing to the poor quality of the data. It is generally thought, however, that data concerning "reserves" and "resources" are considerably biased on the high side. Over the past couple of decades regional estimates of both reserves and resources have been downgraded quite dramatically in some instances. Only estimates of "proved" recoverable reserves can be used when evaluating global coal supplies. Of these total global reserves, some 81 percent are found in just six countries (in descending order): USA, Russia, China, India, Australia, and South Africa (Coal Research 2007). It is thought that coal production will continue to increase up to 2020, will then plateau, peak around 2025 at a level 30 percent higher than current levels, and then begin an inevitable decline (Zittel and Schindler 2007). This is regarded as a "best case" scenario. Of course, the ability of the coal industry to supply an exponentially growing demand for energy will be complicated by the interventions of the mitigation engineers. As with oil, it is highly doubtful that coal will be in a position to support civilization as we know it if we are locked into the old industrial technological paradigm. Those who are more optimistic about the supplies of oil, natural gas, and coal usually make the mistake of underestimating the demand for these resources, which will grow at a rapid exponential rate over the next generation, as China, India and the rest of Asia continues to develop rapidly.

We have also begun to see land being diverted from the production of timber and food to the planting of biofuel crops. This is an echo of the situation in Western Europe during the mid-eighteenth century, when land for human food crops was being diverted to growing oats to feed the rapidly increasing number of horses, which were the main source of motive power for transport, agriculture, and even manufacturing. In addition, as timber and wood were major sources of construction, machinery manufacture, heat, and thermal power, the rapid growth of European societies was effectively eliminating accessible forests and increasing the cost of employing this essential resource in the pre-industrial era. Only the occurrence of the Industrial Revolution removed this pressure on the natural environment, reduced costs of production, and raised standards of living.

So it will be in the first half of the twenty-first century. As the industrial technological paradigm is progressively exhausted, costs of fossil fuels will continue to rise, long-run economic growth and living standards will stagnate and even begin to decline by the middle decades of this century. In turn this situation will generate the incentives – indeed the imperative if we hope to survive and prosper – to introduce an entirely new technological paradigm. This will not be a gradual development, but will involve a quantum leap for human society, most likely taking place within the generation following the middle of the twenty-first century. While the earlier Paleolithic, Neolithic, and Modern (Industrial) Revolutions also involved quantum leaps, the rate at which this has been occurring along the technological development path is increasing exponentially.

The new technological paradigm will completely transcend any of the low-carbon technologies that are currently in operation or even on the drawing board, as these "alternative" technologies are all part of the old industrial technological paradigm. The situation will be similar to the way the technology of the Industrial Revolution completely transcended the "alternative" technologies of wind and water mills – alternative to the use of animal and human power – of the existing neolithic paradigm.

What will this new technological paradigm involve? Nothing that we can currently envisage or image. Here is what I said about the forthcoming technological paradigm shift back in the early 1990s.

> What will the fourth technological paradigm bring? To answer this question would be like attempting in 1750 to say what would unfold from the Industrial Revolution. While there were signs to be read in the mid-eighteenth century, such as the growing use of fossil fuels, there was no way to tell where it would all end. Yet we can speculate sensibly about a central feature of all economic revolutions – the source of energy. The first revolution saw the extension of human energy with the use of more efficient tools; the second revolution saw the partial substitution of animal, water and wind energy for human energy; and the third revolution saw the substitution of thermal energy based upon fossil fuels for both human and animal energy. It appears highly likely that the fourth revolution will involve the substitution of solar energy for fossil-fuel energy. This will resolve, for all practical purposes, the problem that increasing entropy … might ultimately pose for the dynamics of human society. From the fourth revolution, physical constraints upon growth will be limited only by the flow of solar energy. (Snooks 1996: 430)

I called this fourth technological paradigm shift the "Solar Revolution". And throughout this essay, the term "Solar Revolution" has been employed only in reference to the fourth technological paradigm shift, not (as some have mistakenly done recently) to the low carbon technologies that have emerged from the old industrial technological paradigm.

A key question is: Where will the Solar Revolution take place? In *The Dynamic Society* (Snooks 1996: 225–27, 434) I argued that technological revolutions have occurred in "funnels of transformation", which can be thought of as geographically or economically constrained regions at the center of an exhausting technological paradigm. These regions are characterized by heightened competition, higher population interaction, greater pressure on natural resources, and greater exchange of ideas. These funnels of transformation – these regions in the vanguard of technological revolution – have included the Rift Valley of eastern Africa for the hunting revolution; the Fertile Crescent (Old World) and the Mesoamerican isthmus (New World) for the agricultural revolution; and the western edge of Europe for the Industrial Revolution.

What of the forthcoming Solar Revolution? The dynamic-strategy theory suggests that the future technological revolution will take place where the strategic pursuit is most advanced and least restricted by a command mitigation system; where pressure on natural resources is most intense; where investment in deep scientific research and innovation is highest; and where economic growth is based on an internally generated dynamic process (as opposed to an externally dependent process). The initial losers, even in the developed world, will be those countries that intervene most in the operation of their dynamic life-system; that adopt command mitigation economies; that fail to realize the current pressure on natural resources is a function of the approaching technological revolution; that do not regard deep scientific research as their top investment priority; that rely on external forces to drive their economies; and that take the advice of metaphysical economists (neoclassical) and scientists (climate mitigationists) seriously. Countries such as Australia, while affluent, fall into the loser category (Snooks 2008c; 2008d).

The Solar Revolution will not only transform human society, it will make the "need" for climate-mitigation policies totally redundant. But this will only occur if we refrain from the massive intervention being proposed by climate-change scientists and interventionist economists such as Nicholas Stern. Mitigation like that advocated in the *Stern Report* will distort the human life-system at both the national and global levels; will lock in the old paradigm's low-carbon technologies; will keep us captive in an exhausted technological paradigm that is no longer capable of generating economic growth; and will provide regional strongmen with highly tempting incentives to pursue the only alterative dynamic strategy to technological change – the strategy of conquest. This sequence of outcomes, which would follow directly from a rigid adherence to a thorough program of climate mitigation, would generate massive dynamic costs that Stern and other climate-change economists have completely overlooked in their comparative-static framework of analysis. It is time, therefore, to measure these dynamic costs of climate mitigation.

THE DYNAMIC COSTS OF CLIMATE MITIGATION

The impact of mitigation

The key argument in this section is that a determined global effort to impose a comprehensive climate-mitigation program on all nations would cause at least a delay in the emergence of the fourth technological paradigm shift – the real Solar

Revolution. Why? Because, in effect, the dynamic life-system will be hijacked by the mitigation engineers. Instead of strategists responding *creatively*, as they always have done, to the life-system's strategic demand (Snooks 2008a), they will be forced to respond *mechanically* to a set of artificially imposed goals. Goals based on metaphysical values rather than existential realities. An attempt will be made to achieve these antistrategic goals by imposing a large number of major government interventions in the form of a carbon tax/trading system, together with a wide range of directives, incentives, financial manipulations, public preferences, propaganda (called "education") and persuasion (eventually coercion?) required to force the adoption of low-carbon technologies. As shown in Chapter 3, there will also be an attempt to manipulate consumer demand and behavior as well as what is produced and how it is produced.

Owing to this web of centralized controls at both the national and international levels, the global community will be locked into a range of "alternative" (to fossil burning) technologies that are a less economical component of the old industrial technological paradigm. As these low-carbon technologies become more efficient they will extend the dying agony of the old exhausting paradigm and, together with the mitigation command system firmly in place, will prevent the emergence of the new technological paradigm – the real Solar Revolution. By redirecting and constraining the global dynamic life-system, the Masters of Mitigation will also divert and derail the process of scientific development. The reason, as I show in *Dead God Rising* (Snooks 2009: ch. 7), is that science has no momentum of its own; it is a response to the changing strategic demand generated by the dynamic life-system. In the absence of mitigation measures, however, the rapidly rising costs of the old fossil-fuel technologies, the rapid reduction in rates of return on capital invested in these technologies, and the stagnation in growth rates will cause a change in our dynamic life-system and generate a powerful incentive to invest in an entirely new technological paradigm – just as happened in the late eighteenth and early nineteenth centuries in Western Europe as the old neolithic paradigm exhausted itself.

The mitigation engineers, if they can immediately press their plans into action, will cause the global economy to stagnate from the middle decades of the twenty-first century. In effect, the nirvana of neoclassical economics – global equilibrium – will be achieved. But not for long. What my forty-year study of human society has shown is that societies within a competitive environment that do not continue to grow, either collapse or are taken over by more dynamic countries. As the mitigation economy is to be an experiment on a global scale, there will be an attempt to eliminate competition between countries, which may prolong the death throes of human civilization at least until the end of the twenty-first century.

Mitigation and revolution scenarios

We are now in a position to consider two very different scenarios for the twenty-first century that have been generated by the dynamic-strategy theory, and to measure their dynamic costs and benefits. The alternative scenarios are:

- *Mitigation Scenario.* This is the scenario that would unfold if the climate-mitigation programs of the IPCC and the *Stern Review* were fully implemented over the reminder of the twenty-first century. The dynamic-strategy theory suggests that the Mitigation Scenario involves moderate world GDP (WGDP) growth (3.0% p.a.) until 2025, owing to the investment opportunities provided by the low-carbon technologies despite higher energy costs; slower growth (1.0% p.a.) between 2025 and 2050, owing to greater government intervention (and, hence, greater market distortion) imposed on the progressive exhaustion of the industrial technological paradigm; and virtual stagnation (averaging 0.5% p.a.) between 2050 and 2100, owing to the global mitigation economy being captured by an exhausted paradigm. Hence, growth of WGDP in the Mitigation Scenario slows dramatically once the investment opportunities provided by the low-carbon technologies have been fully exploited; and progressive stagnation is the outcome of being locked into the old exhausted industrial paradigm because of: (a) the shackles imposed by a command mitigation economy; (b) the distortion of the dynamic life-system; (c) the reduction of pressure driving the technological revolution owing to the premature reduction of greenhouse-gas concentrations; (d) the reduction of revolutionary pressure owing to the inevitable slow-down in the economic development of the lesser-developed world under the global mitigation command economy; and (e) the diversion and derailment of scientific progress owing to an artificially constrained life-system. Remember, it is assumed that a full-on mitigation program will be in place throughout the remainder of the twenty-first century.

- *Revolution Scenario.* This scenario, as suggested by the dynamic-strategy theory, involves a modest, but declining, growth of WGDP (averaging out at 3.0% p.a.) until 2025, owing to the initial but increasing signs of paradigm exhaustion. This deceleration process is expected to continue more dramatically between 2025 and 2050 (averaging out at 1.5% p.a.). By the middle decades of the twenty-first century our model suggests that the old industrial paradigm will be completely exhausted. Around 2050 – give or take a decade – the new technological paradigm – the Solar Revolution – kicks in and WGDP grows rapidly and exponentially owing to the sudden opening up of radically new strategic opportunities (averaging 5.0% p.a., which is a conservative rate similar to that achieved between 1950 and 1973: see Maddison 2003: 260) until 2100, and beyond. The rate of growth of WGDP under the new technological paradigm starts from a low base around 2050 (owing to its restriction to the pioneering societies), but grows exponentially thereafter, as it takes hold and spreads quickly around the globe.

Both the Mitigation Scenario and the Revolution Scenario generated by the dynamic-strategy theory are very different to the conventional growth scenarios suggested by the historicist and neoclassical general *equilibrium* (i.e. static) models, which have been modified to include assumptions about climate change by IPCC, Stern, Garnaut, and others. The conventional scenarios *considerably overestimate* the growth of the mitigation (or command) economy, as they completely overlook the lock-in effect of an exhausting/exhausted industrial technological paradigm (even one modified by low-carbon technologies); and they *massively underestimate* the growth of the non-mitigation (strategic or free enterprise) economy, because their models cannot capture the technological pathway or the technological paradigm shift. The *Garnaut Review* (2008) spells out its "assumptions" concerning the growth of WGDP: it over-optimistically expects WGDP to peak at 4% p.a. in the early 2020s; and even more optimistically expects it will fall no lower than 2.5% p.a. by 2075, and 2.0% by 2100. Like Stern and the IPCC, Garnaut does not recognize the progressive constraining influence of the old exhausting technological paradigm up to the about 2050, and a totally exhausted one thereafter.

Figure 5.1a **World GDP under Mitigation and Revolution scenarios, 2007 to 2100: geometric scale ($US billion)**

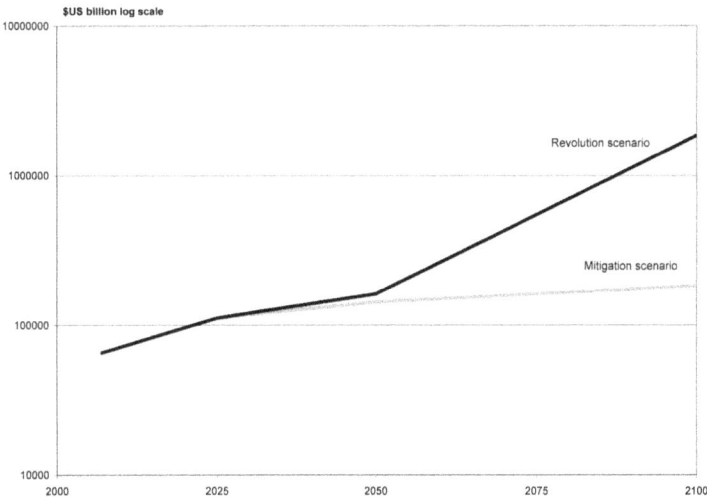

Sources: 2007 world GDP level from the CIA World Factbook, PPP weighted.
Projections are author's own calculations.

Figure 5.1b **World GDP under the Mitigation and Revolution scenarios,
2007 to 2100: Arithmetic scale ($US billion)**

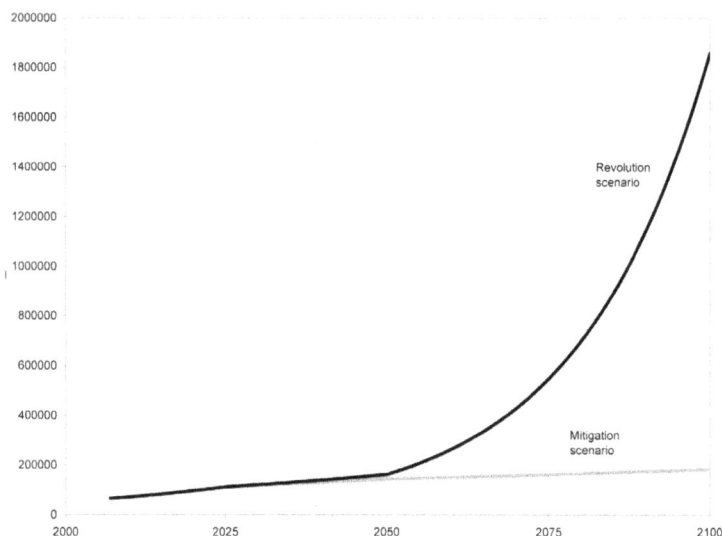

Sources: as for Figure 5.1a.

The outcomes of the Mitigation and Revolution Scenarios are summarised in Table 5.1 and Figures 5.1a and 5.1b (which show these relationships both arithmetically and geometrically). In 2007, the world's GDP in US currency was $65,610 billion (*CIA World FactBook*). In the Mitigation Scenario, WGDP increased moderately to $111,599 billion in 2025; $142,941 billion in 2050; but only to $182,970 billion in 2100 (on the heroic assumption that civilization had not yet collapsed under this command system instituted at the urging of the mitigation engineers). In contrast, the Revolution Scenario experiences a similar increase to $111,599 billion in 2025; a slightly better $161,726 billion in 2050; and then a very impressive $1,850,153 billion in 2100 as a result of the real Solar Revolution. Hence, WGDP in the Revolution Scenario is greater than that in the Mitigation Scenario in 2050 by a modest factor of 1.13 but in 2100 by a massive factor of 10.11.

Table 5.1 **Projected growth of world GDP, 2007–2100 (US$ billion)**

	2007	2025		2050		2100	
	WGDP	**% p.a.**	**WGDP**	**% p.a.**	**WGDP**	**% p.a.**	**WGDP**
Mitigation	65,610	3.0	111,599	1.0	142,941	0.5	182,970
Revolution	65,610	3.0	111,599	1.5	161,725	5.0	1,850,153

Note: These calculations abstract from price changes.
Source: See text

This then is the *real* cost – the dynamic rather than the static cost – of imposing a comprehensive climate-mitigation program on humanity. As shown in Table 5.2, rather than being a modest 1 percent of WGDP per annum, as argued by Stern and other climate-mitigation economists, **the real cost of a full-on mitigation program would be at least a worrying 12 percent by 2050, and a massive 90 percent by 2100**. And it would continue to increase into the twenty-second century as the global mitigation economy begins to disintegrate owing to antistrategic oppression and military conflict. So, what appears to be a modestly costly insurance policy in the static virtual world of neoclassical economics, is in the real dynamic world a total disaster from which we might never recover. Unless it is aborted before it gets this far. Even so, any delay in the emergence of a new technological paradigm will be very costly: each year we delay will cost between 12 and 90 percent of WGDP, depending at what point the command mitigation economy is dismantled. And, of course, it will take years to recover from the collapse of the mitigation economy, just as it has for Russia following the collapse of the USSR. While the human cost was tragically high in the USSR, this will be dwarfed by the imposition and collapse of the global mitigation economy in the twenty-second century.

Table 5.2 **Costs of climate mitigation – dynamic versus static**

	Static costs (Stern) (% of WGDP)	Dynamic costs (Snooks) (% of WGDP)
2025	1.0	0.0
2050	1.0	11.6
2100	1.0	90.1

Source: see text.

The choice of futures, therefore, is a critical one. By adopting the course of action proposed in this essay (see Chapter 6), and abandoning the comprehensive mitigation program proposed by the IPCC, Stern and the other mitigation engineers, *before it gets underway*, the world will save approximately US$27.7 quadrillion. This is an enormous sum of money – 28 million, billion US dollars (or 28 followed by 15 zeros) – and is represented graphically by the triangular area between the two curves in Figure 5.1a. **To put this in a context we can more readily understand: at the 2007 level of world GDP (WGDP) it would take us 422 years to pay for this mitigation cost.** Surely no rational person, organization, or government would, in the light of these results, be rash enough to want to impose a comprehensive mitigation program on the world. How likely are my predicted mitigation results? I rate these results as "very likely", owing to the proven explanatory and predictive outcomes of the realist dynamic-strategy theory in a wide range of disciplines in the social and natural sciences over the past two decades. Indeed, far more likely than current climate projections, which are based on simplistic historicist models that are unable to take structural change into account.

Figure 5.2 **Carbon dioxide concentrations under Mitigation and Revolution scenarios: 2007 to 2200**

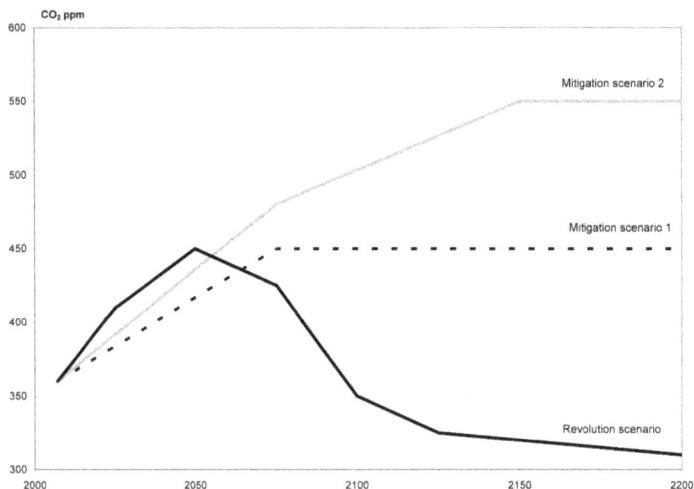

Sources: 2007 C02 ppm level from IPCC. Projections are author's own calculations.

In the face of a forthcoming technological revolution, a mitigation program would not only be incredibly costly, it would be totally unnecessary. The forthcoming technological paradigm shift will release pressure on the environment and radically reduce greenhouse-gas emissions. Figure 5.2 shows schematically the changes in carbon dioxide concentrations in the atmosphere expected under both the Revolution and Mitigation Scenarios. The mitigation scenarios for carbon dioxide concentrations are taken from IPCC reports. The Mitigation I concentrations pathway is that expected if the full-on climate-mitigation program is undertaken seriously and immediately on a global scale. It shows CO_2 concentrations rising from present levels of about 350 ppm to about 450 ppm by 2075 and then stabilizing at that level over the next century. The Mitigation II concentrations pathway climbs at a higher rate until it reaches 550 ppm around 2150, and then levels off. Its higher levels are the result of delays in implementing the full mitigation program. Global temperatures are expected to be higher as a consequence of this tardiness.

Figure 5.2 also shows the expected concentrations pathway under the Revolution Scenario predicted by the dynamic-strategy model. Between 2000 and 2050, its levels are expected to be higher than those under mitigation, but, owing to the slow-down of growth, the rate of increase of concentrations between 2025 and 2050 will also slow down. But after 2050 when the real Solar

Revolution kicks in, concentrations will begin to fall, slowly at first but then more rapidly. The present scientific consensus is that current carbon dioxide concentrations can only be reabsorbed into the carbon dioxide "sinks" – the deep oceans and the earth – slowly over the next couple of centuries (Pittock 2006: 12–14). Recently, some scientists have even controversially suggested that this process will take hundreds of thousands of years – that it "will last longer than Stonehenge, longer than time capsules, far longer than the age of human civilization so far"(Archer et al 2009). While the consensus viewpoint is myopic, the controversial viewpoint is essentially defeatist. Fortunately, both viewpoints – *which implicitly assume that future technology (even over the next few hundred thousand years) will be limited to what can be achieved within the current industrial technological paradigm* – are fatally flawed owing to their failure to develop a realist general dynamic theory of society.

More realistically, the dynamic-strategy model suggests that technological breakthroughs (in response to strategic demand) will occur in the area of carbon dioxide absorption, particularly from 2075, as a spin off from the technological paradigm shift. My model further suggests that by 2200 carbon dioxide concentrations (around 300ppm) could approach levels that were experienced in the late eighteenth century (around 280ppm). Even by 2100 they could be in the vicinity of those experienced in the late twentieth century (around 350ppm), which compares favorably with the mitigation level of between 450–500ppm. Temperatures will, with a lag, also follow this rise in the first half of the twenty-first century, but will fall thereafter to levels that by 2100 will be comparable with those in the nineteenth century. Hence, the great irony is that by the end of the twenty-first century carbon dioxide concentrations and, hence, temperatures will be much higher under all versions of the climate-mitigation program than if we follow the dictates of the dynamic life-system as we have always done. **Climate mitigation will make the planet much warmer than if we merely allow the forthcoming technological revolution to take its course**.

Whatever course of action we take, major investment in adaptation programs will be required to minimize the impact of climate change already in the pipeline and as a result of rising greenhouse-gas concentrations to 2050. This will involve expenditures in repairing damage inflicted by more frequent and more severe storms; undertaking capital works to limit the damage from more regular flooding; to invest in greater water catchment, conservation and distribution; to repair drought devastated lands; to enable populations to shift to less flood-prone, drought-prone, fire-prone and storm-prone regions; and to invest in restorative technologies. Most of these expenditures would also have been required under the various mitigation regimes. We know this can be done because our dynamic life-system, which ensures our survival and prosperity, was shaped by large and abrupt climate-change events. Adapting to future climate change will be even more feasible owing to the modern world's greater technical proficiency.

MITIGATION AS AN AGENT OF COLLAPSE

The range of mitigation outcomes summarized in Figure 5.1 is the most optimist version of what will happen in the twenty-first century if the world adopts the comprehensive program advocated by the mitigation engineers. As argued above, a full-on mitigation program will lock us into the old exhausted industrial paradigm from the middle decades of this century, and lead to economic stagnation from which we will be unable to escape. No antistrategic society, especially once it has stagnated, as it inevitably will, can last for long.

The USSR is an excellent example of a society hijacked by antistrategists, which totally lost its way. As the goals, directives and incentives were determined metaphysically (in response to philosophical ideas) rather than strategically (in response to the life-system via strategic demand), the USSR lost all direction, became increasingly inefficient and unproductive and, within the space of just seven decades, collapsed. In the pre-industrial era when conquest was an economic strategy, Russia and its satellites would have been invaded and taken over by other more viable European countries.

A similar fate awaits the global economy hijacked by the mitigation engineers. In a world dominated by antistrategic goals and incentives – a world in which the strategists are unable to respond to strategic demand generated by the dynamic life-system – the only option for those wanting to survive and prosper will be for regional strongmen to defect from the climate-mitigation regime, and to pursue the only dynamic strategy available to them – war and conquest. This will bring them into conflict with the leaders of the global mitigation society, which will be backed up by multi-national military forces. In effect, the mitigation engineers will plunge us all back into the conditions that dominated the pre-Industrial Revolution era.

Why is this so? In a world where technological revolution and population increase are blocked by the Masters of Mitigation – the political leaders of the global mitigation society – the only way of generating economic expansion is through war and conquest. There are no other dynamic strategies that can be employed for this purpose. Needless to say, war and conquest is a zero-sum game, in which the victors gain at the expense of the vanquished. And in an era of nuclear weapons, it could even be an end game.

While a world that ends in Armageddon is an improbable outcome, it is not an impossible one. It will depend on how determined the Masters of Mitigation are to impose their metaphysical values on the world and whether they have been able to gain complete political control. It would probably take the emergence of a mitigation dictator to get this far. Improbable? Yes. Impossible? No. Who in the late 1920s and early 1930s believed that the author of *Mein Kampf* would ever become dictator of Germany or that he would be able to bring continental Europe to its knee? Dictators emerge out of economic chaos and insecurity, and a full-on mitigation policy would certainly produce these conditions on a global scale. Even the ephemeral financial crisis of late 2008 and early 2009 – which has been talked up to a global recession by the usual doomsters – has led to the re-emergence of the metaphysical interventionists. At the recent (February 2009) World Economic Forum at Davos, the German chancellor Angela Merkel and the British prime minister Gordon Brown advocated the establishment of a UN economic council modeled on the Security Council to "police" the global economy and to "enforce" new standards of finance on individual nations. The states represented on the council would become "the guardians of economic and social order". Chancellor Merkel insisted that the world requires "clear-cut rules quite in contrast to an unfettered capitalism", which should be "enshrined in the form of a global economic order charter". If large-scale global intervention can re-emerge at merely the *hint* of economic recession, imagine the reaction if climate change does cause substantial *actual* dislocation.

Possibly more realistically, an unfolding Mitigation Scenario would lead to a growing realization in saner societies that this policy was distorting the global dynamic system and leading the nations of the world into real and deep economic crisis. This might be sufficient to result in some nations defecting from the climate-mitigation cabal, possibly with the use of force. While this might not lead to collapse, it would certainly result in a much-delayed emergence of the real Solar Revolution – probably beyond 2100 – which would cost humanity dearly (as suggested in Table 5.1). Climate mitigation or technological revolution? The choice is ours, and it will certainly be a critical choice.

Chapter 6
What's to be Done?

The world has arrived at a major crossroad. We are considering embarking on the greatest and most dangerous adventure in our entire history. And we are thinking of doing so on the flimsiest of information and knowledge. While the science of climate change is reputable and impressive, the message it has delivered is clear but concerning: we can only understand how climate will change in the future if we understand the dynamics of human society, owing to the influence of human activities on global warming. This is concerning because the traditional social sciences are unable to explain the dynamics of human society.

Without a realist general dynamic theory of human society the social sciences are unable to deal with the big issues of life, such as human-induced climate change. Consequently they have no idea how human society and human activity will unfold over the next century. Hence, the traditional experts cannot tell us how human-induced climate will change during this period. This is hardly a good basis from which to launch a comprehensive climate-mitigation program – a program that will entail massive government intervention in the global economy, including the distortion of the market mechanism and the employment of centrally determined directives and incentives, direct government involvement, the exercise of preferences for low-carbon technologies and producers, and the use of propaganda and persuasion to change consumer habits. Such a poorly researched and risky enterprise can only be regarded as totally reckless.

WHAT'S BEHIND THIS RECKLESS ADVENTURE?

Humans possess an inherent fear of the future, together with a compulsion to intervene in the world to ensure that it doesn't collapse. Today this fear has manifested itself not only in relation to climate change, but also to the current (October 2008) ephemeral financial "crisis". As I argue in a recently (2008) completed book, entitled *Dead God Rising*, the early emergence and development of a belief in superhuman guardians was the outcome of this instinct to survive and prosper. It was recognition that, while we humans don't understand the dynamic life-system that ensures our survival and prosperity, we do understand that in the past this system has broken down many times. The ruins of earlier societies are all around us. So, if we don't understand how this life-system works and what is needed to sustain it, then we need to seek out those superhuman guardians who do. Every society in the history of our species has invested heavily, with both time and resources, in religions designed to gain the support of these special guardians or gods. Every society in the history of our species has looked to specialized professionals – the "priestly philosophers"

– who claim to understand the ways of the guardians, gods, or forces of fate. In the past, these were the shamans, wisemen, and priests; today they are the climate scientists and orthodox economists. What these priestly philosophers have in common is their belief in metaphysical ideas based on a deductive methodology. As such, it contrasts with the realist ideas derived from empirical observation employed in this essay. When it comes to the big issues facing the future of humanity, it is all a matter of faith not science, owing to their failure to develop a science of societal dynamics.

With the emergence of the dynamic strategy of technological change at the time of the Industrial Revolution, science rose to replace religion as a means not only of understanding our world but also of influencing it so as to maintain order and stability. We believe that, armed with science, we can dispense with the old gods. Investment in science – the social as well as the natural variety – is now considered a better way to ensure the stability of our world.

Unfortunately this is not so. Science is unable to provide a better understanding of the dynamic life-system today than religion was able to do in the past. Certainly science has provided us with considerable knowledge about the physical, natural, and human worlds, but it hasn't been able to show us how they work as dynamic systems. What it has provided, however, is greater confidence in ourselves. This is a double-edged sword. Once, we believed in the guidance of gods, now we believe in our own wisdom and abilities to reform the world. The *irony* is that our understanding of the dynamic life-system is, in orthodox hands, no better today than it has ever been; and the *danger* is that we believe the opposite.

We need only recall the confidence with which orthodox economists have entered the knowledge-free zone of climate mitigation to advise governments about launching the world on this reckless adventure. We have seen that economists are perfectly happy to employ their static, short-run, marginal theory, together with simplistic historicist models, to make judgments about the complex dynamics of human society. With a naive cheerfulness they tell us, in effect, that even if this great adventure fails it won't cost us much.

But as I've attempted to show above, orthodox experts are not in a position to estimate the costs of a mitigation program if they have no real idea of what it is that they are mitigating. How is it possible to estimate the costs of something when we don't know how it will unfold in the future? We desperately need a realist dynamic theory about the structural changes our society is currently undergoing and will undergo in the future. Only then can we estimate the dynamic as opposed to static costs of climate mitigation. As I show in Chapter 5, the dynamic costs are massive.

THE INEVITABLE FAILURE OF LARGE-SCALE INTERVENTIONS

It is essential to consider how large-scale, if not global, interventions have turned out in the recent past. As mentioned earlier, the largest and most risky of interventions in the past was the establishment of the command system of the USSR. This experiment – which was massively expensive for the Russian people and their satellites in terms of time, resources, and lives – collapsed after a mere three generations. The reason for this collapse was that the Marxist interventionists, who devised this command economy, knew nothing about the dynamics of their life-system. As I explain in *The Ephemeral Civilization* (1997) they ignored it, abused it, and the Russian people and their neighbours paid the cost.

Another major series of metaphysical interventions can be seen in the economic and political manipulation of the lesser-developed world. In *Global Transition* (1999) I show that the "development industry" has little understanding of the real nature of the development process, which I call the "global transition" – a process by which the underdeveloped countries on the periphery are gradually drawn into the "strategic core" of interacting developed countries. This is also the process by which the development potential revealed by the last technological paradigm shift – the Industrial Revolution – is gradually and predictably achieved (see Figure 4.2). This, in other words, is the predictable dynamic mechanism by which the old technological paradigm is exhausted and the new one emerges.

Not understanding this realist and predictable process, the development industry believes the material advancement of poorer countries can only occur through its interventions. The curious facts are that while the development industry has existed only for about half a century, societal material progress has been taking place along an exponential development path for the past two million years. During this time, as we have seen, there have been three global transitions and paradigm shifts. And between the Industrial Revolution (1780–1830) and the emergence of the development industry in the mid-twentieth century, a large number of countries passed through the development process without any "expert" advice. If anything, the development industry has slowed down the current process of global transition through its inappropriate and self-interested interventions. Interestingly, the development industry only emerged when European colonialism declined, suggesting that it is a way the developed world can exercise a degree of control over the less-developed world in a post-colonial era under the guise of altruism. Of course not all, or even a majority of, participants in the development industry have other than the best, if misguided, motives; the same cannot be said, however, for the rich countries financing this industry.

Further, there are many examples of interventions in Third-World countries by international organizations, such as the IMF and World Bank, which have been responsible for creating economic and social chaos. In *The Global Crisis Makers* (2000), I show that these international organizations have been employed by the developed world to impose their own inappropriate neoclassical economic policies – such as the deflationary and system-distorting policy of inflation targeting – on Third-World countries desperately seeking international aid. Also, through the WTO, these same countries are attempting to force neoclassical free-trade principles on poorer countries even though at a similar stage of economic development they employed tariff protection as a strategic instrument. These international organizations have made international aid and trade concessions conditional on the adoption of economic programs that undermine the dynamic life-systems of lesser-developed countries. While the developed world is wealthy enough to pay the cost of Neoliberal policies, lesser-developed countries are not, and, if they take these policies seriously, usually descend into economic chaos and war. This has been the case in countries such as Yugoslavia and Rwanda.

My point is that modern interventions in the world generally fail because the metaphysically influenced interventionists have no idea how the underlying dynamic life-system operates. The examples I've provided demonstrate the considerable economic and social costs that flow from these ill-advised interventions. Interventions based on ideas and philosophies that have little contact with reality. Yet, as costly as these interventions have been, they are only a trial run for the massive global intervention being planned by the mitigation engineers. I have provided compelling theoretical/empirical reasons for believing that the global climate-mitigation program will fail spectacularly, will cost human society massively in terms of lost WGDP, and could, if pursued relentlessly, lead to the global collapse of civilization as we know it. But the greatest failure of climate mitigation will reside in the fact that it will be to no avail, because greenhouse-gas emissions and concentrations under mitigationist policies will be much higher than if we just got on with the next technological revolution.

THERE IS A PLACE FOR POSITIVE ACTION

There is, of course, a role for human remedial action. What we can and must do is to come to a thorough understanding of the dynamic life-system that enables us to survive and prosper. Instead of studying human society in a short-term, static framework, we need to come to grips with the way our dynamic system works. The dynamic-strategy theory presented in Chapters 4 and 5 is a good way to start this process. Once we understand the system, which has been driving human society for the past 2 myrs and life for the past 4,000 myrs, we will be in a position to optimize the progress of civilization and the betterment of the natural world by removing obstacles to its effective operation. Obstacles that include inappropriate interventions – regarding societal goals, price systems, incentives, and technologies – formed by other-worldly ideas and philosophies.

It is essential to be sensitive to the requirements of the dynamic life-system, particularly to strategic demand. As we have seen, this is the demand generated by the unfolding dynamic strategy for a wide range of strategic inputs such as factors of production (land, labor and capital), institutions (societal rules), organizations (social networks), together with ideas of all types including those of a technological, cultural and strategic nature. In the process of this creative interaction between strategic demand and the agents of supply, appropriate goals of society – those ensuring survival and prosperity – will be established. Any barriers to the free working of this strategic demand-response mechanism, such as inflation targeting, should be removed. There is one particularly important area where proactive policy will be beneficial, and that is government investment in the *general* infrastructure of science and technological change. We know from the dynamic-strategy theory that the future of humanity will be dependent on the pursuit of the dynamic strategy of technological change; and we know that the next technological paradigm shift is imminent. The sooner the new technological revolution occurs, the lower will be the costs of climate change and environmental damage. What is required here is not gambling on any *particular* technological pathway, as that will be determined by individuals and companies responding to strategic demand, but investment in the generation of new knowledge through appropriate scientific, higher educational, and research facilities. A doubling of the current levels of GDP devoted to these activities in the immediate future would be a good start.

While humans are good at responding to what has happened, we have great difficulty acting in anticipation of something we think might happen. We rarely understand the consequences of our interventions. This is how we have developed genetically as a species – by responding to strategic demand – as explained in my book *The Selfcreating Mind* (2006). Accordingly, investment in "adaptation" policies and programs, as well as remedial technologies, is a sensible way to go.

Under the Revolution Scenario outlined in Chapter 5 – see Figure 5.2 – the need for adaptation expenditures will be higher until 2050 than those suggested by the mitigation engineers, but thereafter the need for these policies will fall quite rapidly to 2075, by which time they will have returned to levels lower than today. Even by 2060 the need for remedial action under the Revolution Scenario will be less than that under even the most optimistic Mitigation Scenario (Mitigation I, Figure 5.2).

Although the Revolution Scenario will probably lead to higher carbon dioxide concentrations in the period before 2050, this may not be translated into higher temperatures. As mentioned in Chapter 2, there are highly reputable scientists specializing in research on solar activity, who are convinced that solar activity and output will decline significantly over the next two decades, leading to modest reductions in global temperatures. If this does eventuate, it will fortuitously compensate for any temporary human-induced pressure on climate. And once solar activity increases again, say from the 2030s, we should be in a position technologically to reduce the adverse impacts of warmer temperatures on human society. These technological measures might, as some scientists have suggested, include a combination of space-mounted "sunshades", aerosol particles released into the atmosphere to reflect some of the inflowing sunlight, injection of sequestered carbon dioxide into the ground, and more. Of course, this all comes at a cost, but only a small fraction of the cost of the proposed climate-mitigation program. And it is a cost that we can easily monitor, as it is for *past* damage rather than a gamble on possible *future* damage. But this is not an argument in favor of relaxing our remedial vigilance, which must be conscientiously maintained.

There is an important issue here that should be recognized. Our dynamic life-system is already in the process of correcting the impact we are having on climate, and it is taking place unremarkably without any proaction on our part. Indeed, the impact of climate on our dynamic life-system will hasten this normal corrective action, as the higher costs of doing business under global warming will be reflected in a stronger and more urgent strategic demand for technological transformation that will generate the real solar revolution.

The choices facing us in the opening decades of the twenty-first century are momentous. We can either get in touch with our dynamic life-system – as our species has been trying unsuccessfully to do over the past few hundred thousand years – and commit ourselves to the imminent technological revolution, or we can leave our heads in the clouds and blindly place our faith in a metaphysically inspired, massively interventionist climate-mitigation program. If we choose the path advocated by the mitigation engineers, we will pay a very heavy economic and social price, from which we may find it difficult to re-emerge. Let there be no doubt that today we face a critical choice of futures – a choice which may block out the sun.

Select References

This select list of references provides a brief overview of the general reading material in this field, particularly for the new science of societal dynamics. More detailed and specialized reading lists can be found mentioned in the IPCC reports, the *Stern Review*, and the author's books listed here.

Archer, D. et al (2009), "Atmospheric lifetime of fossil-fuel carbon dioxide", *Annual Review of Earth and Planetary Sciences,* 37 (forthcoming, May).

Bryson, R.A. and G.J. Dittberner (1976), "A non-equilibrium model of hemisphere mean surface temperature". *Journal of Atmospheric Sciences* 33: 2094–2106.

CIA *World Factbook*, 2008.

Coal Research Committee (2007), *Coal: Research and Development to Support National Energy Policy*. Washingto DC: National Academies Press.

Ehrlich, P.R. and A.H. Ehrlich (1990). *The population explosion*. New York: Simon &Schuster.

Energy Bulletin (http://www.energybulletin.net)

Garnaut, R. (2008). The Garnaut Climate Change Review. Draft report. (June). Canberra (www.garnautreview.org.au). International Energy Agency (IEA) reports.

IPCC (2007). Fourth assessment report: climate change 2007. Geneva: IPCC. 4 vols: 1. *Synthesis report*; 2. *The physical science basis*; 3. *Impacts, adaptation and vulnerability; 4. Mitigation of climate change*

Fogel, R.W. (1964), *Railroads and American economic growth: Essays in econometric history.* Baltimore: John Hopkins.

Fogel, R.W. (1989), *Without consent or contract: The rise and fall of American slavery*. New York and London: Norton.

Hirsch, R.L. (2005), Peaking of world oil production: Impacts, mitigation and risk management. A report to the US Department of Energy.

Lovelock, J. (1990). *The ages of Gaia. A biography of our living earth*. Oxford: Oxford University Press.

Lovelock, J. (2006). *The revenge of Gaia.* London: Allen & Unwin.

Maddison, A. (2003). *The world economy: historical statistics.* Paris: OECD.

Meadows, D.H. et al (1972). *The limits to growth.* New York: Universe Books.

Meadows, D.H. et al (1992). *Beyond the limits. Confronting global collapse, envisioning a sustainable future.* Post Mills, Vt: Chelsea Green.

Nazaretyan, A.P. (2005), Snooks-Panov vertical. In Mazow, I.I., et al (eds), *The encylopaedia of global science.* Dialog Raduga: Moscow.

North, D.C. (1990), *Institutions, institutional change, and economic performance.* Cambridge and New York: Cambridge University Press.

Pittock, A.B. (2006). *Climate change. Turning up the heat.* Melbourne: CSIRO Publishing.

Rifkin, J. (200). *The hydrogen economy.* New York: Tarcher/Putman.

Scitovsky, T. (1954), "Two concepts of external economies", *Journal of Political Economy* 62 (2).

Snooks, G.D, (1993). *Economics without time. A science blind to the forces of historical change.* London/Ann Arbor: Macmillan/University of Michigan Press.

Snooks, G.D. (1996). *The dynamic society. Exploring the sources of global change.* London & New York: Routledge.

Snooks, G.D. (1997a). *The ephemeral civilization. Exploding the myth of social evolution.* London & New York: Routledge.

Snooks, G.D. (1998a). *The laws of history.* London & New York: Routledge.

Snooks, G.D. (1998b). *Longrun dynamics. A general economic and political theory.* New York/London: St Martins Press/Macmillan.

Snooks, G.D. (1999). *Global transition. A general theory of economic development.* New York/London: St Martins Press/Macmillan.

Snooks, G.D. (2000). *The global crisis makers. An end to progress and liberty?* New York/London: St Martins Press/Macmillan.

Snooks, G.D. (2002). "Uncovering the laws of global history". *Social Evolution and History* 1: 25–53.

Snooks, G.D. (2003). *The collapse of Darwinism, or the rise of a realist theory of life*. Lanham, MD & Oxford: Lexington Books, Rowman & Littlefield.

Snooks, G.D. (2005). "The origin of life on earth: a new general dynamic theory". *Advances in Space Research* 36: 26–34.

Snooks, G.D. (2006a). *The selfcreating mind.* Lanham, MA & Oxford: University Press of America, Rowman & Littlefield.

Snooks, G.D. (2007). "Self-organisation or selfcreation? From social physics to realist dynamics". *Social Evolution and History* 6: 118–44.

Snooks, G.D. (2008a). "A general theory of complex living systems: exploring the demand side of dynamics". *Complexity* 13 (July/August): 12–20.

Snooks, G.D. (2008b). "The irrational 'war on inflation': why inflation targeting is both socially unacceptable and economically untenable". Global Dynamic Systems Centre *Working Papers*, no. 1 (March). [IGDS website]

Snooks, G.D. (2008c). "Australia's long-run economic strategy, performance and policy: a new dynamic perspective". *Economic Papers*, 27 (September): 208–32.

Snooks, G.D. (2008d). "Recession, depression, and financial crisis: Everything Economists want to know but are afraid to ask". Global Dynamic Systems Centre *Working Papers*, no. 7 (October). [IGDS website]

Snooks, G.D. (2009a). "The new global crisis makers: Economic intervention and the loss of strategic leadership". Global Dynamic Systems Centre, *Working Papers,* no. 9 (February). [IGDS website]

Snooks, G.D. (2009b). *Dead God Rising. The Role of Religion and Science in the Universal Life-System* (forthcoming).

Suzuki, D.T. and A. Gordon (1990). *It's a matter of survival*. Sydney: Allen & Unwin.

Stern, N. (2005). *Growth and empowerment: making development happen.* Cambridge, Mass: MIT Press.

—— (2007). *The economics of climate change. The Stern Review*. Cambridge: Cambridge University Press.

Zittel, W. and J. Schindler (2007), Crude oil: The supply outlook. A report to the Energy Watch Group (Germany). Ottobrunn Germany.

About the Author

Graeme Donald Snooks is the Executive Director of the Institute of Global Dynamic Systems (IGDS) in Canberra. For twenty-one years between 1989 and 2010 he was the foundation Coghlan Research Professor in Economics in the Institute of Advanced Studies at the Australian National University. More than two decades ago he embarked on an ambitious research program to develop a realist dynamic theory of the changing fortunes of human society and life from their beginnings. This has given rise to the widely acclaimed dynamic-strategy theory (recently published in *Advances in Space research* and in *Complexity* the journal of the Santa Fe Institute), which Professor Snooks is employing to rethink all aspects of the life sciences. This is the first general dynamic theory in the history of human thought to employ an effective demand-side approach. The significance of this is that all supply-side theories are fundamentally flawed.

The results of this research have been published in a number of well-received trilogies, including the global history trilogy (*The Dynamic Society, The Ephemeral Civilization,* and *The Laws of History*), the social dynamics trilogy (*Longrun Dynamics, Global Transition,* and *The Global Crisis Makers*), and the dynamics of life trilogy (*The Collapse of Darwinism, The Selfcreating Mind,* and *Dead God Rising*). Future volumes will explore the dynamic nature of human values and will provide an overview of the entire research program. The core discovery of this work is the universal life system, analyzed for the first time in the last-mentioned book.

About IGDS Books

IGDS Books is the imprint of the publishing activities of the Institute of Global Dynamic Systems in Canberra. As Executive Director of the Institute, Professor Graeme Snooks oversees the activities of IGDS Books.

For information about the Institute or IGDS Books, see the Institute's website, or contact Professor Snooks at seouenaca@gmail.com.

For information and orders about the Institute's publications – books and working papers – please contact the Institute Administrator at institutegds@gmail.com.

www.ingramcontent.com/pod-product-compliance
Lightning Source LLC
Chambersburg PA
CBHW070903280326
41934CB00008B/1564